cooking
for your kids

joshua david stein

cooking

for your kids

at home with
the world's
greatest chefs

✳ **vegan**

♦ **vegetarian**

🥛 **dairy-free**

🌾 **gluten-free**

🕞 **30 minutes or less**

🫙 **5 ingredients or less**

introduction

Parenting is, as any parent will tell you, messy and hard, and, for most of us, a little improvisatory. It's an exhausting business, the rearing of our young, and doesn't stop even when they're no longer that young. I've been a parent for the last eight years and the child of one for my entire life. At no point have the demands eased, they've just changed.

Less often put into words, but no less true for it, is that raising a child can be tremendously rewarding, that love is the ample ballast to the strain. Often these moments of reward—at least when your kids are as young as mine, eight-year-old Achilles and seven-year-old Augustus—are momentary and take place around a kitchen table or in the kitchen itself. These jewel-like benedictions happen while making pancakes on Sunday mornings, in the precious pax between sibling quarrels about who gets the first one off the griddle. (Don't tell your first-born, but the first one off the griddle is always a bit wonky.) They are just as likely to happen side by side while julienning vegetables or in the glorious powdery chaos of baking bread. They cannot be forced and rarely submit to planning. However, by cooking with your child and for your child, you create auspicious conditions for them to arise.

Sometimes, however, the kitchen isn't a refuge. For many parents, myself included, the dinner table can be a battlefield. Each meal is a skirmish, a jostling of control as we parents seek to nourish our young and our young seek to nourish their sense of self by refusing nourishment. A mouth to feed is the same mouth that refuses to open, save to angrily reject food. We resort to ultimatums and threats—by "we" I mean, of course, I—negotiating episodes of *Teen Titans Go!* for bites of carrot and lettuce. For most of my career as a food writer, I've come home to a child who eats only chicken makhani takeout, homemade pizza (without the sauce), and a bakery's worth of bread. Meals became so contentious that I even wrote a children's book—which became children's books—about the joys of eating, simply to be able to present food, which I loved, without the power struggle, which I hated.

But, in either case, joy or strife, who better to turn to for ideas than professional nourishers of soul and body: chefs?

For many chefs, the childhood kitchen is the cave of dreams, the place where the passion for food that has dictated their lives was first ignited. One does not become one of the world's greatest chefs (and thereby included in these pages) if one has not followed one's passion in life. Sure, as any chef will tell you, there are aspects of the job that are less than dreamy. No one fantasizes about P&L tables or food cost calculations. But by and large chefs at this level—and I hope all levels—get to do what they love for a living. There can be nothing better than that, and when my sons tell me what they want to be when they grow up (a game designer and an animal doctor/construction worker/game designer, respectively) I say, "Well, I hope you get to do what you love." And I mean it. I get to do what I love, which is write cookbooks like this one, and I hope they are as fortunate as I have been.

Every writer, chef, and parent with whom I've spoken feels the same way I do.

But chefs are a special case. It is a supreme irony that although chefs love feeding people, they rarely have time to feed the people they love. Such are the vicissitudes of running a restaurant—especially during trying times—that more often than not, as in six out of seven days, a chef is in his or her restaurant kitchen during those magical mealtime moments that form the source material for their own livelihoods. And so, like so many parents around the world, they do the best they can: perhaps rushing home before dinner service to make a quick meal; rising at the crack of dawn, despite crawling into bed but a few hours before, to make breakfast and maybe lunch simultaneously; carving out sacred days, often Sundays, when there's nothing planned except cooking at home and visits to the farmers' market. Chefs being chefs, and parents naturally being problem solvers, they've devised shortcuts, hacks, efficiencies, and strategies to get delicious food onto their family tables.

These recipes reflect both the passion of chefs as parents and a harvest of their professional expertise for home use. As it turns out, the same skills work just as well for one or two very choosy clients as they do for a restaurant full of them. Often, what chef parents bring home isn't simply know-how but actual ingredients. Such is the case with Danny Bowien, whose son, Mino, loves the overnight brisket of Mission Chinese, albeit in different form (page 158), or Elena Arzak's children, Nora and Matteo, who delight in an apple masquerading as an onion (page 208), a favorite both at home and in the dining room of her restaurant Arzak. This is, perhaps, the greatest perk of being the child of a chef. (My own father, who worked in pharmaceutical R&D, used to bring home leeches.)

Among the other benefits is having a parent passionate about and skilled in communicating culture through food. We become who we are around the tables of our childhood. And there is perhaps no more clear transfer of knowledge than family recipes. The dual role, taken seriously by most parents but rarely as consciously, is to provide nutrition for our children's growing bodies but also for their budding selves, as citizens and members of a community. Whether it is Slovenian *jota* (page 190) or Greek *dakos* (page 62) or a Mexican-American albondigas-inspired meatloaf (page 174), the recipes in this volume are the nutrients that allow these young eaters to grow roots.

Finally, chefs make delicious food. Just as a tax accountant—at least a scrupulous one—doesn't gum up his returns, a chef doesn't switch off his or her taste buds once at home. In fact, in this world of aversions and inversions, allergies and intolerances, chefs have become nimble navigators of the menu, subtle suitors of substitution. For those of us who have picky eaters at home, we could do much worse than follow if not the exact recipes then the fleet-footed logic of chefs whose recipes resemble shelves (modular, affordable, versatile). Throughout these pages you'll find ample passive time but little active prep. You'll find recipes ripe for freezing, portioning out, and reheating when needed. Wherever possible, you'll find suggestions for leftovers. These recipes are precise, if you want them to be, but won't complain if a few liberties are taken. These chefs know their children; you know yours.

But mostly what you'll find is a group of highly skilled, highly motivated parents around the world stretched as thin as a piece of chewing gum between work and family and trying to do what they love for those they love. In this chefs aren't alone, of course, but they are singularly equipped to help the rest of us.

*

For most of us, there is no meal more variable in length and ambition between weekday and weekend than breakfast. During the week, breakfast falls during peak hustle. School beckons, work calls, stress abounds. Breakfast is slotted in like a wooden shim between morning responsibilities and getting out the door. Breakfasts on Saturdays and Sundays, on the other hand, loop leisurely like telephone wires, sun streaming through windows, cartoons playing in the other room, a frying pan sizzling with eggs or pancakes.

But for chefs, breakfast is relatively immune from the rhythms of the weekday squeeze and weekend leisure. Since many work late into the night six nights a week—or very early into the morning—and since many of the world's best restaurants are open only for dinner service, breakfast is the rare moment a chef can enjoy cooking at home with his or her family. At breakfast, the chef can finally let loose in the home kitchen. It is testament to the enduring—and almost hegemonic—grip of the breakfast canon that, despite this freedom, chefs and their children, like the rest of us, go in so heavily for eggs and pancakes, porridge and toast. Breakfast is a companion unparalleled in its constancy. Naturally, tastes change with time, but breakfast is almost immune from evolution.

More so than any other daily meal, parents and children find common ground at the breakfast table. What a child eats, a parent eats. When that child becomes a parent, the cycle continues. Yet this isn't meant to suggest breakfast is either static or boring. Indeed quite the opposite. Breakfast is the perfect place to gently expand palates.

Whether this is in Asma Khan's *khageena* (page 14) or the shrimp seasoning in custardy *gyeranjjim* (page 12) made by Beverly Kim's mother that she now makes for her children, the comforts of breakfast can be the Trojan horses of adventure.

These breakfasts form the underpainting for a lifetime of culinary exploration. Of the few memories I have as a child in the kitchen with my father, his pancakes—formed into the shape of a snail, sizzling on a skillet—play a central role. I hope my own sons remember the *aebleskivers* of their youth, the perfectly round Swedish pancake balls important enough to justify their own pan, stuffed with a raspberry for Auggie and chocolate for Achilles.

Now that they're of ages to start cooking themselves, it is with the relatively forgiving eggs that they have started. It's hard to truly turn an egg inedible, so they're perfect for young hands. Tentatively turning the knob of the range, painstakingly cracking the shell, solicitously attending to the solidifying albumen, engaged as the yolk breaks open and that, too, hardens, and inordinately proud to find self-sufficiency, my children are discovering the joys of cooking through breakfast. (Of course, neither actually eats the eggs they make. That task falls to me. Cholesterol be damned.)

When done right, even the most rushed breakfast is an apt reminder that we are all children in the morning. We greet the sunrise with fresh eyes and, hopefully, are beckoned to the table and toward the challenge of the day, by the smells wafting from the kitchen.

*

breakfast

beverly kim and johnny clark

steamed eggs

Serves 4

2 cups (400 g) Korean short-grain rice
3 medium dried anchovies
2 teaspoons toasted sesame oil
6 eggs
4 tablespoons finely julienned carrot
4 tablespoons finely sliced scallion (spring onion)
2 tablespoons minced onion
2 tablespoons saeu-jeot juice
4 teaspoons toasted sesame seeds
1 teaspoon dried chili threads (optional)
¼ teaspoon salt
¼–½ teaspoon fish sauce
Kimchi, for serving

Equipment
Steamer
Medium ceramic bowl

"

When Daewon was a baby, we used to rinse kimchi to get rid of the spice and feed it to him. Now he loves the flavor.

"

Since both Beverly and I [Johnny] work almost 24/7, breakfast is really the time when we can cook for the family. As a girl, *gyeranjjim*, or Korean steamed eggs, was one of Beverly's favorite dishes. Her mother would make a huge bowl and the whole family would dip in to take a share of it. Paired with a hot bowl of rice, the silky umami flavor of the eggs—cleverly filled with thinly sliced vegetables if desired—is tremendously comforting. The salted shrimp seasoning called *saeu-jeot* (available at any Asian grocery store), together with toasted sesame seeds, gives the dish its signature depth of flavor. That Daewon, our eldest, requests *gyeranjjim* makes us so happy because we see that our cultural heritage is becoming his. At Parachute, we've made elevated versions of this dish— adding foie gras or truffles—but at its heart, these steamed eggs remain a child-friendly comforting breakfast.

•

In a bowl, soak the rice in cold water to cover for at least 30 minutes and up to 2 hours. (This can be done the night before.) Rinse and cook according to the package directions.

In a saucepan, soak the anchovies in 1½ cups (12 fl oz/350 ml) water for 20 minutes. Bring to a boil, then reduce and cook for 10 minutes. Strain the broth (discard the anchovies) and let cool.

Grease a medium ceramic bowl with 1 teaspoon of the sesame oil with a paper towel. Set up a steamer and bring the water to a boil.

Meanwhile, in another medium bowl, whisk together the eggs and cooled anchovy broth until smooth. Add the remaining 1 teaspoon sesame oil, the carrot, scallion (spring onion), onion, saeu-jeot, sesame seeds, chili threads (if using), and salt until fully incorporated.

⌂ PARACHUTE,
WHEREWITHALL
(CHICAGO, ILLINOIS, US)
•
☺ DAEWON, 10; HANUL,
3; BOWIE, 1

breakfast
<u>breakfast</u>
steamed eggs
↓

<u>dinner</u>
lentil bolognese
with spaghetti squash,
↳ p. 148

Transfer the egg mixture to the ceramic bowl. When the steamer is ready, place the ceramic bowl inside and cover. Steam until the eggs are set, 14–16 minutes.

Serve communally with hot Korean rice and kimchi on the side.

asma khan | spicy scrambled eggs

2 tablespoons vegetable oil
2 large white onions, chopped
3 large tomatoes, chopped
3 fresh green chilies, chopped
1 teaspoon ground turmeric
½ teaspoon chili powder
8 eggs, lightly beaten
½ teaspoon salt
Chopped cilantro (coriander),
for garnish

"

I try not to make mealtimes battle-grounds or to be impatient when my children refuse food, even though it can be frustrating. Despite weaning both my sons similarly, they have developed very different food prefe-rences. I avoid praising the child eating the food as the 'good' one—since that often makes things worse, and I try to leave long gaps before retrying a dish or flavor that has previously failed.

"

Khageena, or spicy scrambled eggs, is a great way to introduce the flavors of green chilies with something children already find familiar and comforting, eggs. The level of spice is also adjustable. While portioning out *khageena*, simply avoid the chilies and children will taste only a gentle hint. I've always liked making this dish for my own children as it felt special having a "grown-up" breakfast with their parents, even when they were quite young. This was my way to encourage them to eat with my husband and me on weekends. My older son would often help to beat the eggs. When he finally went off to university, the first thing he did was send me a picture of *khageena* he had made.

•

In a frying pan, heat the oil over medium-high heat. Add the onions and fry until they are translucent. Add the tomatoes and fresh chilies and cook for 3–4 minutes, until the tomatoes soften.

Add the turmeric and chili powder and stir for 30 seconds. Pour in the beaten eggs and cook gently, stirring until you achieve a soft set. Season with the salt, then check the seasoning as you may need to add more.

Serve the eggs warm, garnished with cilantro (coriander).

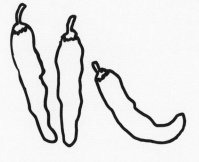

🏠 **DARJEELING EXPRESS**
(LONDON, UK)
•
☺ **ARIZ, 20; FARIZ, 15**

<u>breakfast</u>
spicy scrambled eggs
↓

<u>lunch</u>
spiced potatoes
with peas
↳ p. 80

reuben riffel

herbed mascarpone scrambled eggs

Serves 4

1 bunch fresh thyme, leaves picked
1 teaspoon superfine (caster) sugar
1 teaspoon flaky sea salt
4 cups (800 g) halved Rosa or cherry tomatoes
Olive oil
2 cups (450 g) spinach leaves, stemmed
Salt and freshly ground black pepper
12 slices pancetta
8 eggs
2 heaping tablespoons mascarpone
2 tablespoons (30 g) unsalted butter
5 tablespoons grated Parmesan cheese

Smoked salmon, thinly sliced, for serving
Croissants or toast, for serving (optional)

Though I've finally figured out my daughter's palate, my son is still quite fussy. Often what we make goes uneaten. Thankfully both my wife, Maryke, and I enjoy this breakfast, so if Max doesn't, there's more for us. (Recently, however, he's hardly left us with any leftovers.) The eggs were originally inspired by my love of tiramisu, in which mascarpone cheese pays a key part. One day, I substituted the cheese for cream in my scrambled eggs and it worked amazingly well. The addition of spinach, tomato, and thyme gives the breakfast a healthier, more savory note that sets the tone for the rest of our day.

•

Preheat the oven to 350°F (180°C/Gas Mark 4).

In a small bowl, mix together the thyme leaves, sugar, and salt. Arrange the tomatoes on a sheet pan, season with the sugar/salt/thyme mixture, and leave to cure for 10 minutes. Transfer to the oven and bake for 8 minutes. Set aside to cool to room temperature. Leave the oven on.

Pour a little olive oil onto the bottom of another sheet pan, and arrange the spinach in a single layer without overlapping them too much. Season with salt and pepper and roast until crispy, about 10 minutes.

Place the pancetta on a baking tray and bake for 10 minutes, until crispy as well. Meanwhile, crack the eggs into a bowl and add the mascarpone. Stir the mixture slowly, just until the yolks break.

🏠 **REUBEN'S RESTAURANT & BAR (JOHANNESBURG, SOUTH AFRICA)**
•
☺ **LATIKA 10; MAX, 7**

breakfast
herbed mascarpone
scrambled eggs
↓

lunch
pork and beans
with orzo
↳ p. 98

Slowly heat the butter in a cold nonstick frying pan. Once the butter starts to bubble, add the egg mixture and fold slowly until the egg starts to set. Fold in the spinach and tomatoes until well incorporated. You are looking for a soft texture.

Season to taste, sprinkle with the Parmesan, and serve with the pancetta, salmon, and croissants or toast (if using).

japanese omelet with cheddar and formula

sean brock

Serves 1

2 eggs
½ cup (4 fl oz/120 ml) baby formula
1 tablespoon (15 g) unsalted butter
¼ cup (25 g) grated sharp Cheddar cheese
Salt

Equipment
Nonstick 7½ × 3½-inch (19 × 9 cm) tamagoyaki pan

My wife, Adi, and I are obsessed with Japan. We took Leo there when he was only six months old. Every chance we get we make him Japanese food, preparing his palate for our next trip. Which I perpetually hope is soon. This recipe is a combination of a *tamagoyaki*-style Japanese omelet with a French one. The result is a no-mess omelet—relatively no mess, that is—that Leo can eat with his hands.

•

Preheat the tamagoyaki pan over medium heat while you mix the eggs. Crack the eggs into a bowl and whisk in the cold formula. Whisk until well emulsified.

Remove the pan from the heat but leave the burner on. Add half the butter, allow to melt, and evenly coat the pan. Add the eggs and set the pan back on the burner. With a silicone spatula, stir the egg mixture vigorously for 45 seconds and then remove from the heat once again. Allow the egg mix to settle evenly, then sprinkle the Cheddar on one half. Return to the heat and carefully roll the omelet into a rectangle toward the handle. Add the remaining butter and remove from the heat. Continue to press and shape the omelet into a compact rectangle.

Remove from the pan and drain on a paper towel. Finish with some salt and cut into 1-inch (2.5 cm) chunks to serve.

TAMAGOYAKI PAN

⌂ AUDREY
(NASHVILLE,
TENNESSEE, US)
•
☺ LEO, 1

breakfast
japanese omelet with
cheddar and formula
↓

snacks
kabocha squash with
oats and apples
↳ p. 102

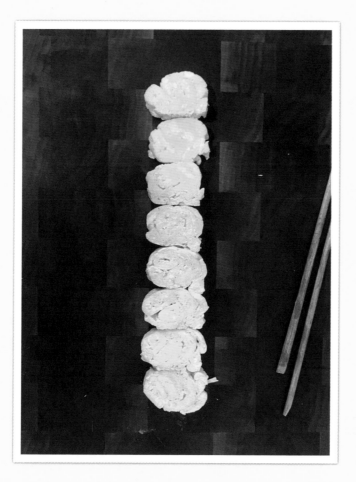

nick roberts and brooke williamson

egg in a hole with crispy prosciutto and broccoli pesto

Serves 4

For the prosciutto:
4 large slices prosciutto

For the broccoli pesto:
1 cup (90 g) broccoli florets, steamed but still crunchy
Large handful of fresh basil leaves
1 clove garlic, peeled
½ cup (45 g) grated Parmesan cheese
Pinch of salt
½ cup (4 fl oz/120 ml) olive oil, plus more if needed

For the egg in a hole:
4 slices country white bread, at least 1 inch (2.5 cm) thick
3 tablespoons (45 g) unsalted butter
4 eggs
Salt and freshly ground black pepper

Egg in a Hole, Toad in a Hole, Bird in a Nest, Egg in a Nest. There are many names for this classic breakfast preparation. It's all my son wants to eat. I have to plead with him to have cereal twice a week. Hudson was never a huge fan of bacon, but he fell in love with prosciutto when we traveled to Italy two years ago. And I love the crunchiness of my ham, which reminds me of the toasted Black Forest ham sandwiches my father used to make. The best part, as any kid knows, is the buttery toasted center, which perches atop the hole like a delicious manhole cover.

•

Crisp the prosciutto:
Preheat the oven to 375°F (190°C/Gas Mark 5).

Arrange the prosciutto on a baking sheet and roast until crispy, about 15 minutes. Let cool slightly, then break into pieces.

Meanwhile, make the broccoli pesto:
In a food processor, combine the broccoli, basil, garlic, Parmesan, and salt and pulse until they are finely chopped. In between pulses, slowly pour the olive oil in until combined. Scrape down the sides of the bowl, and add more oil if it needs it to achieve a pesto-like consistency.

Make the egg in a hole:
Using a ring mold cutter or a knife, cut out a round from the center of each slice of bread about 3 inches (7.5 cm) in diameter.

Heat a griddle or large nonstick frying pan over low heat. Add the butter to melt, then place the bread—along with the cut-out hole—into the butter, flipping to coat both sides evenly in the melted butter. Crack an egg into the middle of each slice of bread and season with salt and pepper.

🏠 HUDSON HOUSE,
THE TRIPEL, PLAYA
PROVISIONS
(LOS ANGELES,
CALIFORNIA, US)
•
☺ HUDSON, 12

breakfast
egg in a hole with
crispy prosciutto
and broccoli pesto
↓

treats
fresh plum, black sesame,
and vanilla sour belts
↳ p. 206

"

I [Brooke] had Hudson after I'd been cooking in professional kitchens for over ten years. I was not planning on getting pregnant when I did, but decided to roll with it, because who knows when I'd ever actually feel ready. My husband, Nick, and I opened Hudson House when Hudson was one year old, and I remember having a tremendous amount of guilt about how much time I was spending away from him. I felt overwhelmed every time I left him, that I wasn't a good parent when at work, or that I wasn't a good businessperson when at home with my child. I could do nothing right. There was a period of time when Nick and I would be at work from 10 a.m. to 3 a.m., with one sitter taking over for another, and Nick and me trading off nights of sleep. Never in my dreams did I imagine not being around to raise my own child. Certainly I am not alone in feeling that I couldn't do anything right. We stuck Hudson in preschool the moment he was old enough, and I cried at every drop-off. But now, twelve years in, I've got a well-adjusted kid who's with us ninety percent of the time and can adapt to any given situation. He's flexible, easy to travel with, and just a wonderful all-around human being. I wouldn't trade any of it for better timing.

"

When the egg is slightly set and the bottom of the bread is golden brown, about 3 minutes, use a metal spatula to flip the bread gently to ensure you don't break the egg. Season the other side with salt and cook for another 2 minutes, depending on how well done you like your eggs.

To assemble:
Place the egg in a hole (and the cut-out round) on a plate. Garnish with a large spoonful of broccoli pesto and some crispy prosciutto.

za'atar egg salad sandwich

Serves 2

For the egg salad:
4 eggs
2 tablespoons za'atar
1 tablespoon olive oil
1 teaspoon salt
½ bunch fresh oregano, leaves picked (about 2 tablespoons)

For the quick-pickled onions (optional):
½ medium red onion, thinly sliced
1 teaspoon salt
¼ cup (2 fl oz/60 ml) apple cider vinegar

For the sandwiches:
4 slices bread, toasted
½ cup (10 g) arugula (rocket)

Zain is obsessed with za'atar and eats it by the mouthful. He was born in Oakland, but his palate is definitely one of an Arab child. He loves dipping his bread in olive oil and then za'atar. But to get protein in his diet I decided to boil eggs and mash them in the mix, like my grandma, or *tayta*, used to do in Southern California by way of Lebanon. This egg salad sandwich recipe is a mix of boiled egg, za'atar, olive oil, salt, and fresh herbs. You can serve it open-faced on toast or in a pita pocket breakfast sandwich, the way Zain eats it. For adults, I add pickled red onion, labneh, arugula (rocket), and hot sauce for an extra kick, as we serve it in the restaurant, in a house-made sesame bread.

•

Make the egg salad:
Set up a bowl of ice and water. Bring a small pot of water to a boil over medium-high heat. Using a slotted spoon, carefully lower the eggs into the water one at a time. Adjust the heat to maintain a gentle boil and cook for 6½–7 minutes, depending on your desired yolk consistency (I like it jammy!). Transfer the eggs to the ice water and chill until just slightly warm, about 2 minutes.

Peel the eggs immediately and cut into quarters. Place in a medium bowl with the za'atar, olive oil, salt, and oregano. Mix and mash with a fork until well combined.

Make the quick-pickled onions:
Place the onion in a bowl. In a cup, combine the salt, vinegar, and ¼ cup (2 fl oz/60 ml) water and stir to dissolve the salt. Pour over the red onion. Let sit for at least 10 minutes then drain.

Assemble the sandwiches:
Top the toasts with the egg salad, arugula (rocket), pickled onion (if using), and any kind of fun topping you desire.

adeline grattard

spicy crab omelet

Serves 4

8 eggs
Salt
2 tablespoons sunflower oil
7 oz (200 g) crabmeat
1 tablespoon soy sauce
4 chives, minced
½ teaspoon sambal oelek
Freshly ground white pepper

(30)

When I was living with my husband, Chi Wah Chan, in Hong Kong, we used to have this omelet quite often for breakfast. Now that we live in Paris with our children, it makes sense for us to share the memories from our time in Hong Kong with them. Since I spend such long hours in the restaurant at night, we love to take the time in the morning to cook together, although this omelet can be enjoyed pretty much for any meal Of the day.

•

In a bowl, whisk the eggs and 2 tablespoons water with a pinch of salt. In an 8-inch (20 cm) frying pan, heat the sunflower oil over medium-high heat until shimmering. Add the eggs, crab, soy sauce, chives, and sambal oelek and season with white pepper. Cook the omelet until just barely set. Fold and serve immediately.

🏠 YAM'TCHA,
CAFÉ LAI'TCHA (PARIS,
FRANCE)
•
☺ NINA, 13; SAM, 8; LEON, 3

breakfast
spicy crab omelet
↓

lunch
tomato and smoked
tofu salad
↳ p. 70

vegetable frittata

Serves 4

For the frittata:
½ white onion, sliced
2 tablespoons extra-virgin olive oil
Sea salt
¼ cup (2 fl oz/60 ml) coconut water
½ zucchini (courgette), sliced into coins
Dash(es) of sherry vinegar
½ head radicchio, torn
5 eggs
1 tablespoon milk
½ cup (45 g) grated Gruyère cheese
1 tablespoon (15 g) unsalted butter

For assembly:
3 tablespoons (45 g) unsalted butter
4 slices levain bread
½ bunch arugula (rocket)
Juice of 1 lemon

Family mornings are always a great time to eat together. If I wake up early enough I can throw a frittata together before my daughter leaves for school. Otherwise I save it for lazy weekends. A frittata can literally be anything, so it is the perfect pantry essential. It's also hard to go wrong with a frittata. Overdone, underdone, a little burnt . . . it's always great.

•

Make the frittata:
In a small frying pan, slowly cook down the onion. Start dry, then add 1 tablespoon of the oil and lightly salt. When softened, add the coconut water and reduce until dry.

Meanwhile, in a second small frying pan, heat the remaining 1 tablespoon olive oil and quickly sauté the zucchini (courgette), then season with salt and sherry vinegar. Remove the zucchini (courgette) from the pan and let slightly cool. Meanwhile, add the radicchio to the same pan and allow to wilt. Remove and allow to cool slightly.

In a bowl, beat the eggs with the milk. Stir in the Gruyère, onion, zucchini, and radicchio.

In a medium cast-iron skillet, heat the butter over medium heat until foaming. Pour in the egg mixture and shake it a bit so it doesn't stick. Cook it halfway and flip, or cover, and cook until solid. When just done, invert onto a serving plate and allow to cool for a bit before slicing.

To assemble:
Return the cast-iron skillet to medium heat, add the butter, and melt. Add the bread and griddle until crispy.

Toss the arugula (rocket) with the lemon juice. Serve the frittata alongside the grilled bread and a little arugula salad.

⌂ ROOM 4 DESSERT
(UBUD, BALI)
•
☺ **LOULOU, 15**

<u>breakfast</u>
vegetable frittata
↓

<u>lunch</u>
pasta with chickpeas
↳ p. 150

elena reygadas

black bean molletes

Serves 4

For the mashed black beans:
1 ⅔ cups (300 g) dried black beans
2½ tablespoons cooking oil
½ cup (80 g) diced onion
1½ teaspoons salt

For the green pico de gallo:
7 oz (200 g) green tomatoes, diced
⅓ cup (50 g) diced onion
½ small (4 g) serrano pepper, minced (with seeds)
¼ cup (5 g) cilantro (coriander) leaves, chopped
2 tablespoons fresh lime juice
1 tablespoon olive oil
½ teaspoon salt

For the molletes:
4 Cemitas (recipe follows), split open and lightly toasted
5½ oz (160 g) queso fresco, crumbled
1 medium avocado, peeled, pitted, and sliced
½ cup (20 g) purslane

Molletes are one of Mexico's most special breakfast dishes: an open-faced sandwich laden with black beans and topped with melted cheese. *Molletes*—like *tortas*, *pambazos*, *cemitas*, and *pan dulce*—belong to that long overlooked genre of bread-based Mexican dishes. (We have so much more than tacos and tortillas!) For my daughters' Lea and Julieta's black bean *molletes*, I use *cemitas*, a traditional Mexican soft bread—made with *piloncillo*, which we make in my bakery La Panadería. (The *cemitas* recipe makes a baker's dozen, and you can use the leftover buns for sandwiches and snacks all week long.) I also like to add some avocado and green tomato pico de gallo on top for the acidity. The beans here are an important ingredient because they give the meal a lot of nutrients, which is especially good for my kids, who don't eat a lot of meat.

•

Make the mashed black beans:
Place the beans in a bowl with water to cover by several inches. Let soak for 8 hours.

Drain the beans and place in a pot with 7¼ cups (1.7 liters) water. Bring to a gentle boil and cook until tender, approximately 1½ hours. Drain.

In a saucepan, heat the oil and onion over medium heat and cook until the onion is translucent. Add the beans and mash until you get the consistency of a purée. Season with the salt.

Make the pico de gallo:
In a bowl, combine the green tomatoes, onion, serrano, cilantro (coriander), lime juice, olive oil, and salt and mix well.

Assemble the molletes:
Preheat the broiler (grill) or oven to 500°F (260°C/Gas Mark 10).

breakfast

⌂ ROSETTA,
LA PANADERÍA,
LARDO, CAFÉ NIN
(MEXICO CITY, MEXICO)
•
☺ LEA, 13; JULIETA, 11

breakfast
black bean molletes
↓

snacks
mamey shake
↳ p. 104

Makes 13 rolls

½ cup (85 g) piloncillo or brown sugar
4 cups (500 g) all-purpose (plain)
flour, plus more for sprinkling
1 oz (25 g) sourdough starter
7 oz (200 g) eggs
¼ cup (50 g) sugar
3¼ teaspoons (10 g) active dry yeast
3 tablespoons (45 ml) milk
⅓ cup (70 g) lard or cooking oil, plus
2 tablespoons for brushing
1¼ tablespoons (8 g) freshly ground
anise seed
1¼ teaspoons salt

Set the bread on a baking sheet. Spread the black beans onto the bread and add the crumbled queso fresco on top. Run under the broiler, or bake in the oven, until the cheese is slightly melted. Serve with green pico de gallo, avocado, and purslane atop.

•

Cemitas

Place the piloncillo in 5 tablespoons (75 ml) water over low heat, constantly stirring until you get a syrup. Let cool.

In a bowl, combine the syrup and all of the remaining ingredients. Make circles with a wooden spoon to mix well. Knead until you get an elastic dough. Let the dough sit at room temperature in a covered container until it doubles in size, approximately 1½ hours.

Punch the dough down. Divide the dough into 13 portions of a scant 3 oz (80 g) each, then shape with your hands into round buns.

Brush lightly with oil, and sprinkle each bun with some flour. Arrange on a baking sheet, cover with a cloth, and let sit at room temperature for approximately 1 hour.

Preheat the oven to 350°F (180°C/Gas Mark 4) with steam, or place a pan with water on a lower rack.

Bake the rolls until they feel light and are golden brown, about 15 minutes.

jocelyn guest
and
erika nakamura

sourdough pancakes

Serves 4

2 cups (260 g) all-purpose (plain) flour
4 teaspoons baking powder
1 teaspoon baking soda (bicarbonate of soda)
2 tablespoons sugar
2 teaspoons kosher (flaked) salt
1 cup (240 g) ripe sourdough starter
1½ cups (12 fl oz/350 ml) unsweetened almond milk
1 egg, beaten
2 tablespoons olive oil
Butter, for cooking the pancakes

"

We never did baby food. We just overcooked stuff and set it out in front of Nina and let her figure it out. We only had to gag her once. We were having a mom-to-mom conversation and weren't paying attention for a moment. She started choking on watermelon, which compresses if you don't swallow it. I [Jocelyn] choked, but I [Erika] leapt over the counter. It was all okay and over in a matter of seconds. It took a while after that, but we got comfortable with the idea of chopping things up and letting her eat alone. The only thing is that we created a monster in that now she only wants to eat what we are eating. This is great, but if we aren't sitting all together at 5 p.m. and having the same thing, she's pissed.

"

By the time we were pregnant with our daughter, Nina, we had moved to the woods in upstate New York from the city. It was winter. As butchers, we weren't natural bakers, but something about being stuck in the woods in winter made me [Erika] want to start making bread. By the time Nina was a few months old I needed to satiate who I was as a chef. Butchering a chicken wasn't really a good option, so I became a zealous starter keeper and sourdough maker. These pancakes are easy to prepare, versatile, and good on the go. Nina loves them. And, unlike many sourdough recipes, the starter here is a flavoring agent, not a fermentation agent, and so there is no waiting involved. With a little more salt, they become a savory snack. With a sprinkle of sugar, they're great for breakfast. Often, I'll cook them all up, load them all up in containers, and take it with me on the road to feed her on the go.

•

In a big bowl, whisk together the flour, baking powder, baking soda (bicarb), sugar, and salt.

In another bowl, mix together the sourdough starter, almond milk, egg, and olive oil. Stir until the ingredients are combined.

Add small amounts of the flour mixture to the wet mixture while stirring well. Continue to whisk slowly until all dry and wet ingredients are incorporated.

<u>breakfast</u>
sourdough pancakes
↓

<u>dinner</u>
beef and kale meatballs
↳ p. 138

Heat a cast-iron skillet over medium heat and grease with
a generous amount of butter. Using a large spoon or a ¼-cup
(2 fl oz/60 ml) measure, pour the batter into the pan and cook
until the surface is dotted with bubbles. Flip the pancakes and
continue to cook for a couple of minutes until they are golden
brown and delicious. Continue making pancakes until you
can't make pancakes anymore, adding more butter as needed.

walter and margarita manzke

german pancakes with yogurt sabayon

Serves 4

For the pancakes:
1 cup (8 fl oz/250 ml) milk
½ cup (65 g) all-purpose (plain) flour
4 eggs
Pinch of sea salt
1 teaspoon granulated sugar
3 tablespoons (45 g) unsalted butter

For the yogurt sabayon:
1 silver gelatin sheet
1 egg
⅓ cup (65 g) plus 1 tablespoon
granulated sugar
1¾ teaspoons rum (optional)
1 vanilla bean, split lengthwise
½ cup (145 g) Greek yogurt
1⅓ cups (10½ fl oz/325 ml) heavy
(whipping) cream

For assembly:
1 cup (150 g) chopped or thinly sliced
peaches, plus more for garnish
Powdered (icing) sugar, for dusting

Though I [Walter] grew up in San Diego, my mom is from Germany and used to make this recipe when I was a kid. We had an orchard with all sorts of trees and I gravitated toward the peaches. Now we live right behind the restaurant in Hancock Park, and sadly there is no orchard. Between running the restaurant together and taking care of our children, we have a solid schedule down. During the week, I'll take the kids to school, then swing by to pick up Margarita and we'll go to work together. At 3:30 p.m., she'll take off to pick them up and then come back for service. Sundays are the best because that is the full day we can spend together. We'll usually go to the farmers' market and, when they're in season, pick up peaches for these crowd-pleasing pancakes, our kids' favorite.

•

Make the pancakes:
In a blender, combine the milk, flour, eggs, salt, and granulated sugar and blend until incorporated. Strain through a fine-mesh sieve to remove any lumps. Let the batter rest for 30 minutes.

Line a plate with parchment paper. In a 10-inch (7.5 cm) nonstick frying pan, melt 1 teaspoon of the butter over medium heat. Pour ⅓ cup (2½ fl oz/75 ml) of the batter into the pan and swirl all around to cover the whole bottom of the pan. Cook over medium-low heat for about 1 minute. Flip the pancake and cook for another 30 seconds on the other side. Slide the pancake onto the prepared plate. Continue cooking until the batter is all used up—4–6 pancakes—adding butter as needed. Set aside as they are done.

Make the yogurt sabayon:
Submerge the gelatin sheet in a bowl of ice water. As soon as it softens, squeeze out as much water as possible and set aside.

breakfast

Fill a saucepan with about 1 inch (2.5 cm) water and bring to a simmer over medium heat. In a heatproof bowl (that can sit over the saucepan without touching the water), combine the egg, ⅓ cup (65 g) of the granulated sugar, and the rum (if using). Whisk until the mixture is light and fluffy, then add the bloomed gelatin and scrape in the vanilla seeds. Whisk to incorporate and set aside to cool.

While the egg mixture is cooling, in a stand mixer fitter with the whisk, combine the yogurt and ½ cup (4 fl oz/120 ml) of the cream and whip until stiff peaks form.

Fold the whipped yogurt–cream into the cooled egg mixture until fully incorporated.

In a clean mixer bowl with the whisk, whip the remaining ¾ cup (6 fl oz/175ml) plus 4 teaspoons cream with the remaining 1 tablespoon granulated sugar until stiff. Fold the cream into the yogurt mixture. Transfer to a covered container and refrigerate until ready to use.

<u>To assemble:</u>
Put a pancake on a cutting board. Put about ⅓ cup (2.5 fl oz/75 ml) of the yogurt sabayon in the middle and spread it a little. Top with the peaches, evenly distributed over the cream. Roll the pancake to form a log, encasing the fruit and cream in the middle. Transfer the roll to an individual plate or serving platter. Fill and roll the remaining pancakes. Dust with powdered (icing) sugar, garnish with additional peaches, and serve immediately.

elisabeth prueitt

david eyres's pancake

Serves 2

4 tablespoons (60 g) unsalted butter
½ cup (65 g) all-purpose (plain) flour
½ cup (4 fl oz/120 ml) milk
2 eggs
Pinch of grated nutmeg
Large pinch of salt
2 tablespoons powdered (icing) sugar
Juice of ½ large lemon

"
I get frustrated that I don't have as much time as I would like to cook with Archer, so I have to work hard to carve out space. When we go camping, for instance, or visiting my parents, or planning a movie night at home. Recently I've started a patio garden and have found that, as our cucumbers or rapini or roma beans ripen, we plan for days what to do with them. After the veggies are picked, Archer and I wash, chop, and cook them together.
"

There are many variations of this pancake, named after the Hawaii-based writer at whose home *New York Times* critic Craig Claiborne first discovered it in 1966. But the pastry chef in me loves the precision and elegance of the one-to-one ratio of flour and milk, which scales up or down flawlessly. I use less butter than the original, rarely add the nutmeg, and always add a big pinch of salt.

•

Preheat the oven to 425°F (220°C/Gas Mark 7).

Heat a 12-inch (30 cm) ovenproof frying pan over medium-high heat for 5 minutes, then add the butter. In a bowl, whisk together the flour, milk, eggs, nutmeg, and salt, leaving the batter slightly lumpy. Pour the batter into the pan, transfer to the oven, and bake until puffed and golden, 15–20 minutes.

Sift the powdered (icing) sugar over the pancake, then pour the lemon juice over. Serve immediately.

⌂ **TARTINE BAKERY (SAN FRANCISCO, LOS ANGELES, CALIFORNIA, US), TARTINE MANUFACTORY (SAN FRANCISCO, CALIFORNIA, US)**
☺ **ARCHER, 13**

breakfast
david eyres's pancake
↓

snacks
quick bread-and-butter
pickled vegetables
↳ p. 110

vladimir mukhin

quark pancakes with cherry sauce

Serves 4

For the cherry sauce:
4 tablespoons (50 g) sugar
3½ cups (500 g) fresh or frozen cherries
1 teaspoon (2–3 g) cornstarch (cornflour)

For the syrniki:
15 oz (440 g) quark or cottage cheese
½ cup (60 g) all-purpose (plain) flour
½ cup (100 g) plus 1½ tablespoons granulated sugar
1½ teaspoons salt
4 eggs

For assembly:
6 tablespoons (80 g) unsalted butter
⅓ cup (2½ fl oz/75 ml) sunflower oil
⅔ cup (130 g) sour cream

Syrniki, or quark pancakes, seems like a very simple dish: quark (or cottage cheese), flour, eggs. But every person has their own take on how to make the perfect fluffy *syrniki*, and every Russian kid has happy memories of how his mom or grandmother cooked *syrniki*. I am no exception. My mom and granny used baked milk, or *toplenoye moloko*, to make their pancakes, and now I do as well for my own children at home. It's a very special Russian product that like quark, resembles a creamier delicate cottage cheese. Once you try it, you will only want to eat *syrniki* like that. But it's quite hard to find, even here in Russia, so a better bet is to use quark or cottage cheese, which still yields both a delicious breakfast and many happy memories.

•

Make the cherry sauce:
Melt the sugar over medium heat in a medium saucepan until slightly caramelized, 8–10 minutes. Stir in the cherries and bring to a boil for 3–4 minutes. Whisk in the cornstarch (cornflour) until the sauce is slightly thickened, then remove from the heat.

Make the syrniki:
Strain the quark through a sieve into a bowl. Sift the flour over the cottage cheese, add the granulated sugar and salt, and mix the ingredients. Beat in the eggs one at a time, stirring the dough until smooth.

To assemble:
In a frying pan, heat the butter and oil over medium heat. Once the butter is melted, scoop in ⅓ cup (60 g) batter for each pancake, cooking until golden on both sides and evenly cooked, 3–4 minutes per side.

Serve the pancakes with sour cream and the cherry sauce.

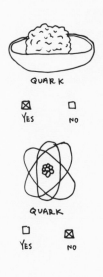

QUARK

☒ YES   ☐ NO

QUARK

☐ YES   ☒ NO

breakfast

<u>breakfast</u>
quark pancakes
with cherry sauce
↓

<u>lunch</u>
zucchini pancakes with
guacamole
↳ p. 88

claudette's famous french toast

Serves 4

For the custard:
1 cup (8 fl oz/250 ml) whole milk
1 cup (8 fl oz/250 ml) heavy (whipping) cream
4 eggs
2½ tablespoons piloncillo or dark brown sugar
1 teaspoon ground cinnamon
¼ teaspoon ground star anise
¼ teaspoon grated nutmeg
Grated zest of 2 lemons
2 teaspoons vanilla extract

For assembly:
6 tablespoons (90 g) salted butter
8 slices Hawaiian bread/challah/brioche
Maple syrup, for serving
Coconut cream, for serving
Fresh berries, for serving

When I was a kid growing up in Tijuana, I remember waking up excited because I could smell my mom making us French toast in the kitchen, or as we called it *pan frances*. She used a leftover French-style sourdough baguette from Guadalajara called *birote*, or softer *torta* rolls called *telera*. Now that I'm a mother, I wanted to include a dish from my childhood that would resonate in my kids' lives as well. I use soft and sweet Hawaiian bread and often make the custard the night before, so the kids wake up to the smell of the bread on the frying pan. The recipe base remains the same as my mother made, but I add little improvisations to clear out fruit from the fridge as needed.

•

Make the custard:
In a blender, combine the milk, cream, eggs, brown sugar, cinnamon, anise, nutmeg, lemon zest, and vanilla and blend until homogeneous. Cover and refrigerate to rest for at least 1 hour and up to overnight. Bring the custard to room temperature before proceeding.

To assemble:
Preheat the oven to 350°F (180°C/Gas Mark 4).

Set a cast-iron skillet or griddle over medium-low heat. Place a dab of butter in the pan, swirling until melted.

Pour the custard into a glass baking dish. Soak the slices of bread, 2 at a time, for 20–30 seconds per side. Once both sides are soaked, carefully remove from the custard, using a slotted spatula if necessary.

breakfast
claudette's famous
french toast
↓

dinner
albondigas-inspired
meatloaf
↳ p. 174

Place the slices in the hot pan (you may need to work in
batches), cooking until golden brown, 1–2 minutes.
Flip and ensure both sides are even. Add butter as needed.

Transfer the slices to a baking sheet and place in the oven
for 5 minutes.

Serve with maple syrup, a dollop of coconut cream, and
fresh berries.

edouarardo jordan

akil's morning oatmeal

Serves 2

1¼ cups (100 g) rolled oats
1½ tablespoons (30 g) agave syrup
⅓ cup (60 g) thinly sliced strawberries
¼ cup (50 g) thinly sliced banana
¼ teaspoon vanilla extract
Pinch of ground cinnamon
⅔ cup (5 fl oz/150 ml) milk
Salt
Scant ¼ cup (50 g) yogurt
Fresh fruit, sliced, for serving

I'm lucky in that Akil tells me what he wants and how he wants it. For instance, he prefers his morning oatmeal in one of two ways: either the brown sugar or the honey version. This recipe is what he calls the honey version—though, as you can see, I use agave syrup as opposed to sugar. My general approach is to give him something with which he is familiar alongside a new ingredient or flavor. He knows to try everything twice, a lesson he learned from us reading the wonderful series of children's books *Kalamata's Kitchen* together.

•

In a small pot, combine the oats, syrup, and 1⅓ cups (10½ fl oz/325 ml) water. Bring to a simmer over medium heat and add the fruit, vanilla, and cinnamon. Cook until tacky and thick, about 3 minutes. Stir in the milk and continue cooking until creamy. Add a pinch of salt and finish.

Divide the oatmeal into two bowls and top each with a spoonful of yogurt and fruit.

breakfast
akil's morning oatmeal
↓

lunch
sunflower butter
and jelly sandwich
↳ p. 60

pierre thiam

fonio coconut pudding with fresh berries

Serves 4

2 cups (16 fl oz/475 ml) coconut milk, or more as needed
1 teaspoon vanilla extract
4 Medjool dates, pitted
Pinch of sea salt
1 cup (140 g) cooked fonio
2 cups (250 g) fresh berries
2 tablespoons cocoa nib or chopped dark chocolate (optional)
Fresh berries, for serving
1 tablespoon unsweetened cacao powder, for serving
Unsweetened shredded coconut, toasted, for serving

In Kédougou, in southern Senegal, we serve fonio to children because of its nutritional properties and because it's easy to digest. Fonio is an ancient grain from West Africa that is gluten-free and particularly rich in two amino acids (cysteine and methionine) that are very important for human growth and are deficient in most major grains. It's perfect for the family because the grain is generous and cooks in 5 minutes. This recipe can be prepared in advance.

•

In a saucepan, bring the coconut milk to a simmer. Add the vanilla and remove from the heat. Measure out 1 cup (8 fl oz/ 250 ml) of the vanilla coconut milk and set aside in a bowl.

Add the rest of the coconut milk to a blender. Add the dates and sea salt and blend on high until smooth and creamy. Transfer the mixture to a large bowl. Fold in ½ cup (4 fl oz/ 120 ml) of the reserved coconut milk. Add the fonio and fold until well combined. Add the remaining reserved ½ cup (4 fl oz/120 ml) coconut milk and fold in.

Gently fold in the cocoa nibs or chopped dark chocolate, if using.

Refrigerate for at least 30 minutes to let the pudding firm up. If it's too firm when you want to eat it, stir in more coconut milk.

Serve chilled with fresh berries, a sprinkle of cacao powder, and/or toasted coconut.

FONIO

breakfast

<u>breakfast</u>
fonio coconut pudding
with fresh berries
↓

<u>snacks</u>
banana beignets
↳ p. 120

whipped lingonberry semolina

Serves 4

9 oz (250 g) fresh or frozen lingonberries (or cranberries)
Pinch of fine sea salt
½ cup (120 g) sugar, plus more for sprinkling
Scant ¾ cup (120 g) coarse semolina
Milk, for serving
⅓ cup (50 g) fresh berries, for serving
Honey, for serving

Whipped semolina is a dish I remember having for breakfast growing up on the west coast of Finland, where lingonberries are common. Now that we live in Ireland, it's a memory I want to impart to my own kids, though often instead of fresh lingonberries we use frozen ones or simply substitute cranberries. It's a fast, convenient breakfast that is sweet but also—thanks to the lingonberries—rich with antioxidants. We enjoy it any time of day: breakfast, lunch, snack, or as a dessert.

•

In a saucepan, combine the lingonberries and 3⅓ cups (27 fl oz/800 ml) water and bring to a boil. Reduce the heat to medium-low and cook until the berries start to break down, about 10 minutes.

Stir in the salt and sugar. Gradually whisk in the semolina and cook, stirring constantly, until thickened noticeably, 8–10 minutes. Taste and add more sugar if desired.

Remove from the heat and let the porridge cool to room temperature. Using an electric mixer, whisk the porridge until light, fluffy, and cool. (The color will turn to light pink.)

Refrigerate the porridge until slightly chilled, approximately 10 minutes. Re-whisk the porridge before serving to get the light fluffy texture. Serve the porridge with a splash of milk, fresh berries, a sprinkling of sugar and honey, if you wish.

breakfast
whipped lingonberry
semolina

↓

dinner
braised cheek of beef,
leftover bread, pickles,
and mashed potatoes

↳ p. 188

daniel rose
and
marie-aude rose

country cheese with blueberries and cream

Serves 4

For the fromage blanc:
4¼ cups (34 fl oz/1 liter) organic whole milk
1 cup (8 fl oz/250 ml) buttermilk
2–3 drops liquid rennet

For serving:
4 tablespoons blueberry jam
8 tablespoons organic heavy (whipping) cream (38% butterfat)

Since we have restaurants on two continents and we both travel a lot, we really make sure to spend as much time together at home as we can when we're both there. Often this is at the breakfast table. I [Marie-Aude] grew up in Paris and Burgundy, but this recipe comes from the Savoie in the Alps. *Fromage blanc de campagne* is the opposite of the skim milk and cereal so many kids have. It fully embraces the hugely fatty and rich dairy but also embodies the French way of eating: high quality in small quantities at the right time of day. *Fromage blanc de campagne* is akin to cottage cheese, but less salty and much creamier. Since we've always had a hard time finding it in the States, I've included a recipe to make your own, though it takes some planning and plenty of time to make.

•

Make the fromage blanc:
Begin by heating the milk to 86°F (30°C): Do this by placing the container of milk in a pot or sink of very warm water. If you do this in a pan on the stovetop, make sure you heat the milk very slowly and stir it well as it heats.

Once the milk is at 86°F, stir in the buttermilk. Then stir in the liquid rennet.

The milk now needs to sit quietly for 24–48 hours while the culture works and the curd forms. The thermal mass of this milk should keep it warm, but during colder months wrapping this in a thick blanket or towel will keep the temperature steady. It is okay if the temperature drops a few degrees during this time.

When the curd is ready, you will notice that it shrinks away from the sides of the pan a bit, and you may see a thin layer of whey on the top. You may even notice some cracks forming on the surface.

breakfast
country cheese with blueberries and cream
↓

lunch
calf's liver "au vinaigre" with sautéed brussels sprouts and bacon
↳ p. 94

Line a colander with fine cheesecloth (butter muslin) and set over a bowl or in the sink. Spoon the curds and whey into the colander and let drain for 3–4 hours. A regular gentle stirring will make sure that the whey drains off. Once it is well drained, you can either whisk it to make it smooth or simply transfer it to a jar to refrigerate overnight.

To serve:
Equally divide the fromage blanc de campagne among four bowls. Top each with 1 tablespoon of blueberry jam and 2 tablespoons of fresh cream.

didem şenol

white cheese and oregano dip on toast

Serves 4

10½ oz (300 g) *beyaz peynir* or white cheese like feta
Juice of ½ lemon
7 tablespoons early-harvest olive oil
Grated zest of 1 lemon
2 sprigs fresh thyme, leaves picked
1 teaspoon dried oregano
Sourdough croutons, toast, or crackers, for serving

Beyaz peynir, literally white cheese, is a breakfast staple here in Turkey. Like feta, it is usually brined sheep's milk, but can be hard or soft. This dip, which comes from my grandfather, uses a soft version. (You can also use regular feta cheese, if you can't find any *beyaz peynir* near you.) What's wonderful about it is you can eat the dip on toast for breakfast or, as my kids also do, as an after-school snack on crackers. With so simple a recipe, the freshness of the cheese and the quality of the olive oil are of supreme importance.

•

In a medium bowl, stir the cheese until smooth. Add the lemon juice and olive oil, whisking to incorporate. When the cheese is smooth and has the texture of a dip, add the lemon zest, thyme, and oregano. Serve on toasted bread or with crackers.

breakfast
white cheese and oregano
dip on toast
↓

lunch
zucchini fritters
↳ p. 124

*

Lunch is not simply the minor leagues of dinner. It is a tent pole meal in itself, midday sustenance for when the mind and body sag like a power line in want of support. Lunch is sui generis, one of the big three, a coequal branch of nutrition. For families, it does share with breakfast a tremendous delta between weekday lunches and weekend lunches. This is owed largely to the fact that, at least during the school year, lunch is a meal our children eat—or don't eat—beyond our gaze, outside of our control, in the company of others. School lunch is perhaps the first time our children's food must compete in the open market with sandwiches, pizza, chicken tenders, French fries (chips), and assorted caloric ephemera. (At least this is the case where I live in the United States, where lunch in many schools is the province of private vendors.) Lunchtime is also when our children's meals are scrutinized by their peers. The so-called "lunchbox moment," the lightning strike of peripeteia, when a child realizes that the smells of his or her kitchen are not universal. For many, this experience can be harrowing. For all it is memorable. We greet our day at breakfast; we reflect upon it at dinner; but at lunch, we are cast headlong in its currents. So lunch is there as a buoy, a reminder of our parents, and the kitchens we call home.

A lunch to be packed is a lunch that must, like our own children, survive the tumble and yaw of a school day. It must be rugged and perseverant. Sandwiches are good, for the bread acts as a natural stabilizer. Importantly they are served at room temperature. Such are the vicissitudes of modern scheduling that many lunches are served preposterously early. (My own son's lunch period is 10 a.m.) And though this defies all common sense, it does mean that, depending on the insulative power of the vessel, fried rices and vegetable stews can survive rather well. Any lunch, in fact, will do as long as it is easily eatable, and can bide its time in a cubby without undue degradation.

But when the weekend rolls around, lunch blooms like a field of wildflowers in spring. Parents and children around the world meet in the kitchen to cook lunch together. For chefs especially, Sunday lunch is a sacred family ritual. With most restaurants closed Sunday and Monday, but most children in school on Monday, Sunday is frequently the only day the family can cook a leisurely meal together. Frequently Sunday rituals include trips to local farmers' markets, be it the Danilovsky Rynok in Moscow or Hollywood Farmers Market in Los Angeles. And when parent and child return to the kitchen, tote bags full of fresh produce, the kitchen becomes a classroom, a child becomes a sous-chef, and lunch is sustenance for not just the family's stomachs but their souls, too.

*

lunch

full moon hotteok

Makes 14 hotteok

For the hotteok dough:
1¼ cups (175 g) sweet rice flour
3 cups (400 g) all-purpose
(plain) flour
1 tablespoon plus 2 teaspoons (20 g)
sugar
3 tablespoons (20 g) corn flour (not
cornstarch/cornflour)
1 teaspoon kosher (flaked) salt
1 egg, beaten
¼ teaspoon vanilla extract
Scant ¾ teaspoon (2 g) active
dry yeast
1⅓ cups (10½ fl oz/325 ml)
warm water
2 tablespoons (30 g) unsalted butter,
cubed and softened

For the filling:
7 oz (200 g) Baek Kimchi (recipe
follows), finely chopped
10½ oz (300 g) 26–30 count shrimp
(prawns), peeled, deveined, and
finely chopped
3½ tablespoons (10 g) minced
perilla leaves
2 tablespoons (20 g) finely minced
yellow or white onion
3 tablespoons (20 g) finely minced
scallions (spring onions)
Salt

For finishing:
1½ tablespoons (20 ml) extra-virgin
olive oil

Hotteok is a traditional Korean street food, a fried yeasted pancake typically stuffed with sugar and chopped nuts and eaten with your hands. Inspired in part by Beijing-style meat pies, we prefer to eat savory versions of *hotteok*. You can sneak all kinds of vegetables into the filling. Here, we use *baek kimchi* (white kimchi), which is not spicy. If you don't have time to make your own *baek kimchi* and can't find it at your local grocer, you can do what Koreans do for their children: rinse off the spicy red chile from traditional *baechu kimchi*. Feel free to play around with the filling ingredients based on what your child loves (or what you wish your child loved)!

•

Make the hotteok dough:
In a large bowl, combine the rice flour, all-purpose (plain) flour, sugar, corn flour, salt, egg, vanilla, and yeast. Using one hand, mix until it resembles coarse sand. Gradually add the warm water, mixing with one hand until it comes together as a dough. Lastly, add the butter and knead it into the dough. Continue kneading until the dough forms a ball. Place the dough back in the large bowl and cover with plastic wrap (cling film) or beeswax wrap. Let rest in a warm spot (ideally 89°F/32°C) until it has more than doubled in size, about 2 hours.

Make the filling:
In a dry frying pan, sauté the minced kimchi for few minutes until the liquid has evaporated. Let it cool.

In a large bowl, mix together the cooled kimchi, shrimp, perilla, onion, and scallions (spring onions). Season with salt to taste.

🏠 **BAROO (LOS ANGELES, CALIFORNIA, US)**

•

☺ **TAIHOON, 7 MONTHS**

lunch
full moon hotteok
↓

snacks
vegetable rice balls
↳ p. 106

<u>Makes 4½ pounds (2 kg)</u>

1 medium head napa cabbage (about 2¼ lb/1 kg), sliced crosswise into 2-inch (5 cm) pieces
Kosher (flaked) salt
1 Korean or Asian pear, peeled, cored, and cut into chunks
1 oz (30 g) garlic, peeled
1–2-inch (2.5–5 cm) piece fresh ginger (10 g)

To finish:

Take 2–2½ ounces (60–70 g) of the dough, roll it into a ball, and flatten with your hands. Place 2 tablespoons (50 g) of the filling in the center of the dough, fold over the dough, and pinch closed. Roll back into a ball and then flatten gently, taking care to repair any tears in the dough.

In a frying pan, heat the olive oil over medium-high heat. Place a few hotteok in the pan and let brown on one side for a few minutes, flattening with a spatula. When the first side is a crispy and light brown, flip and fry on the other side until browned and crispy.

Remove from the pan and enjoy immediately, taking care as there may be hot liquid that escapes when you bite into it.

baek kimchi (white kimchi)

Weigh the cabbage and then measure out salt equal to 3% of that weight. In a large bowl, sprinkle the salt on the cabbage and toss to spread the salt evenly.

In a blender, combine the pear, garlic, and ginger and purée. Line a fine-mesh sieve or chinois with fine cheesecloth (muslin) and set over a bowl. Scrape in the purée and press to get the liquid and strain out the solids.

Sterilize a large container and place the salted cabbage in the container. Add the strained liquid to cover the cabbage and place large bowls with weights in them over the cabbage. Cover the container and leave it at room temperature to ferment for 2–3 days.

pía león and virgilio martínez

pumpkin stew with potatoes and peppers

Serves 6

4 tablespoons vegetable oil
1 white onion, finely chopped
2 cloves garlic, finely chopped
2 tablespoons Peruvian ají amarillo chili paste
1 teaspoon dried oregano
3 macre squash (about 11 oz/300 g each), cut into ¾-inch (2 cm) cubes
¾ cup (110 g) fresh green peas
3 medium potatoes, peeled and cut into ⅓-inch (1 cm) dice
2 medium ears white corn, cut into chunks
½ cup (4 fl oz/120 ml) evaporated milk
¾ cup (160 g) fresh cheese (queso fresco), cut into ¾-inch (2 cm) squares
Salt and freshly ground black pepper
Black olives, for garnish
Cooked rice, for serving

Locro peruano, or Peruvian pumpkin stew, is usually made with a sweet squash called *macre*, which has a savory skin and is endemic to the Peruvian coast. We use it quite often in the restaurant and always—as with most things—reserve a little for home. Of course, since we live so close to the restaurant, and we're there so often, when Cristobal wants to eat or play he comes down, three times a day, to the dining room, the kitchen, or the garden, which also serves as our park and playground. If you have a hard time finding *macre*, which wouldn't be surprising, most pumpkins can be substituted. Cristobal loves this with a side of rice, which accompanies most of his meals.

•

In a medium pot, heat the vegetable oil over medium heat. Add the onion, garlic, chili paste, and oregano. Cook, stirring with a wooden spoon, until the vegetables are browned and softened, about 7 minutes.

Add the cut squash, green peas, potatoes, and corn. Reduce the heat, cover, and slowly cook, stirring every 5 minutes, until the ingredients are tender, about 10 minutes.

Add the evaporated milk and half of the cheese. Let it come to a boil once, then remove from the heat. Season with salt and pepper.

Serve with black olives and the remaining cheese on top, with rice on the side.

lunch

<u>lunch</u>
pumpkin stew with
potatoes and peppers
↓

<u>treats</u>
arroz con leche
↳ p. 200

pía león and virgilio martínez

walter and margarita manzke

adobo fried rice

Serves 4

For the adobo sauce:
3½ tablespoons (50 ml) distilled white vinegar
5½ tablespoons (85 ml) soy sauce
½ onion, roughly chopped
1 tablespoon chopped garlic
1 teaspoon freshly ground black pepper
1 whole star anise
1 bay leaf

For the chicken fried rice:
4 tablespoons extra virgin olive oil
8 tablespoons (120 g) unsalted butter
2 teaspoons chopped garlic
1¼ lb (565 g) chicken breast, cut into ½-inch (1.25 cm) cubes
5 cups (910 g) cooked jasmine rice
Salt, to taste

For assembly:
4 eggs
4 pinches of sliced green scallions (spring onions)
4 oz (115 g) pickled Fresno chilies

Adobo is a staple of the Philippines. It's like our peanut butter and jelly sandwich. I [Margarita] love making this for Nico and Olivia because it connects them to our Filipino culture, even though we live far from my family in Manila. Both kids love this quick and easy lunch, which is pretty rare! Nico's getting better, but for a long time if it wasn't ice cream he wasn't interested. It's also something I can make in the small window I have after I pick them up from school but before dinner service starts at the restaurant.

Make the adobo sauce:
In a bowl, stir together the white vinegar and soy.

In a pot, combine the onion, garlic, black pepper, star anise, bay leaf, and vinegar/soy mixture. Bring to a boil and cook until the onions are translucent. Remove from the heat and let cool. (Adobo sauce can be kept refrigerated for up to 1 week and can be used on everything from chicken to pork to fish.)

Make the chicken fried rice:
In a stainless steel pan, heat the oil and butter over medium heat. Add the garlic and cook until browned. Add the chicken and cook thoroughly. Add the rice, increase the heat to high, and cook the mixture for 3–4 minutes. Add the adobo sauce and stir to coat evenly, cooking for 1–2 minutes to heat through. Salt to taste.

To assemble:
Divide the rice mixture into four serving bowls.

In the same pan, heat more oil if the pan is dry and cook the eggs sunny-side up. Add an egg to each bowl. Top with scallions and pickled chilies.

lunch
adobo fried rice
↓

breakfast
german pancakes
with yogurt sabayon
↳ p. 32

garden "fish" finger sticks

Serves 4

For the breadcrumbs:
1¾ cups (100 g) fresh breadcrumbs

For the "fish" fingers:
7 oz (200 g) sweet potatoes, cut into wedges
2 shallots, peeled and roughly chopped
3½ oz (100 g) carrots, peeled and halved
3½ oz (100 g) beets, peeled and halved
4 tablespoons olive oil
4 cloves garlic, minced
2½ tablespoons (5 g) rosemary leaves
Scant 2 oz (50 g) broccoli, chopped
3½ oz (100 g) fresh peas
Salt

For the dipping sauce:
Juice of 1 lemon
1 tablespoon mayonnaise
2 teaspoons honey
1 teaspoon cilantro (coriander) leaves

For assembly:
4 tablespoons all-purpose (plain) flour
Pinch of freshly ground black pepper
Pinch of smoked paprika
2 eggs
⅛ teaspoon salt
Olive oil, for shallow-frying
4 burger rolls or hot dog buns
Lettuce and tomato (optional)

My daughter, Nur, and I love to make these vegetable "fish" fingers. They're a simple and healthy lunch and offer her plenty of opportunities to help, from forming the veggie mash into fingers to rolling them in breadcrumbs. I try to use the opportunity of cooking vegetables at home with Nur to teach her about agriculture, a subject she doesn't have in school. A tomato has a heart, I tell her, and a history and is part of our story as a people and as a family.

•

Make the breadcrumbs:
Preheat the oven to 350°F (180°C/Gas Mark 4).

Spread the breadcrumbs on a sheet pan and bake until light browned, about 10 minutes.

Roast the vegetables:
Increase the oven temperature to 375°F (190°C/Gas Mark 5).

Toss the sweet potatoes, shallots, carrots, and beets with the olive oil, garlic, and rosemary sprigs. Place the potatoes, shallots, carrots, and beets on a sheet pan, loosely cover with foil, and put in the oven. Spread the chopped broccoli on another sheet pan and put in the oven after 15 minutes. After another 15 minutes, add the peas to the broccoli. Shuffle to toss. After 15–20 more minutes, remove all the vegetables.

Transfer the roasted vegetables to a bowl and use a fork to mash them together, adding salt if needed. Cover and let cool down.

Make the dipping sauce:
In a small bowl, whisk together the lemon juice, mayonnaise, honey, and cilantro (coriander) until well incorporated.

<u>To assemble:</u>

Beat together the eggs with the salt in a small bowl. Roll the vegetable mash into "fish stick" shapes, about 2 inches (5 cm) long and ½ inch (1.25 cm) wide. Lay them side by side on a tray. Cover and refrigerate for 5 minutes.

Pour 3 inches (7.5 cm) olive oil into a frying pan and heat over medium-high heat. Meanwhile, in a medium bowl, sift together the flour, pepper, and paprika. Spread the breadcrumbs on a plate. Dip the vegetable sticks in the egg wash, then in the breadcrumbs, gently shaking to remove excess. Gently place in the oil and fry until golden brown. Repeat until done.

Serve either in burger rolls or hot dog buns with dipping sauce and lettuce and tomato, if desired.

edouardo jordan

sunflower butter and jelly sandwich

Serves 2

2 tablespoons sunflower seed butter
4 slices sourdough bread, cut ¼ inch
(6 mm) thick
3 tablespoons strawberry preserves
1 tablespoon sunflower oil

This is a quick and easy lunch I often make for Akil. It's a step up from the PB&Js I used to eat as a kid. Instead of peanut butter, I substitute sunflower seed butter, which is a healthier and tastier alternative. Also, because there are so many tree nut allergies at his school, the substitution makes it safe for him to bring. The key with so simple a recipe is, as always, quality. A good loaf of sourdough is worth the extra couple of bucks; the preserves should be slightly chunky and without too much sugar. Grilling the sandwich in the pan after it's assembled makes it gooey, crunchy, and delicious, which is why I always make two: one for Akil, one for Daddy.

•

Evenly spread a thin layer of sunflower seed butter over 2 slices of sourdough. Do the same with the preserves. Sandwich the bread together.

In a nonstick frying pan, heat the oil over medium heat. Once hot, add the sandwiches and toast both sides until golden brown. Remove and slice into halves. Serve immediately or let cool and wrap in foil for later.

angelos lantos

cretan salad

Serves 2

4 pieces Cretan dakos
4 tablespoons fresh olive oil
Salt
2–3 tomatoes, finely chopped
or grated
5 oz (150 g) fresh Myzithra cheese
or fresh ricotta
½ teaspoon fresh oregano
2 tablespoons Kalamata olives, whole
1 teaspoon capers
¼ red onion, finely chopped

◊ ㉚

Dakos, the base of this salad, is a Cretan traditional double-baked bread made from barley rusks. It comes from necessity. In the days before refrigeration, double-baking bread allowed it to keep for much longer, good for sailors, shepherds, farmers, and fathers. The use of barley—as well as whole wheat (wholemeal) flour—makes *dakos* one of the healthiest breads available. I love it, too, for its versatility: You can use it as a breakfast bread, as the basis of a salad or dessert, or as here, a sort of panzanella. *Dakos* is the name of the bread, but it is also the name of this salad, which also goes by the name *owl* in Western Crete and *kouloukopsomo* in Eastern Crete, which literally means, "bread for puppies." If buying *dakos* bread in the West, it's often called simply "barley rusks."

•

Wet the dakos lightly with a little water and sprinkle with 2 tablespoons of the olive oil and a little salt. Put the tomato on top, leaving a space in the center for the cheese. Add the cheese and sprinkle with the oregano and salt. Add the olives, capers, and onion. Sprinkle with the remaining 2 tablespoons olive oil and serve.

⌂ SPONDI
(ATHENS, GREECE)
•
☺ MATTHEW, 13;
MANOS, 8

lunch
cretan salad
↓

treats
greek doughnuts with
honey and yogurt
↳ p. 226

suzanne goin
and david lentz

vegetable pistou sandwiches

Serves 4

2 Persian (mini) cucumbers, julienned
1 yellow bell pepper, julienned
1 medium carrot, julienned
6 radishes, thinly sliced
2 tablespoons extra-virgin olive oil
1 tablespoon fresh lemon juice
Salt and freshly ground black pepper
1 baguette
6 ounces (170 g) goat cheese
1 avocado, peeled, pitted, and sliced
3 tablespoons Pistou (recipe follows)
1½ cups (60 g) arugula (rocket)

Alex is our adventurous foodie kid; her twin brother, Jack, is a "turkey and Cheddar, no mayo," and Charles, the youngest, will eat anything. But all three of our kids love bread, baguettes in particular. One summer, I [Suzanne] remember they were on a baguette kick and this was a sandwich variation I made Alex. (Jack stuck with turkey and Cheddar.) Besides being fresh and bright, juicy and satisfying, the prep work needed gave us an opportunity to have the kids involved. We have always tried to include them both around the table and in the kitchen. They would pick herbs, shuck beans or peas, try to peel garlic, and wash greens from their earliest days. It is in these moments we all find ourselves chatting about our lives and telling stories that never seem to come up when you pick them up from school and say, "So honey, how was your day?"

•

In a medium bowl, combine the cucumbers, bell pepper, carrot, and radishes. Add the olive oil, lemon juice, 1 teaspoon salt, and a generous grinding of black pepper.

Halve the baguette horizontally, leaving the two halves attached. Spread the goat cheese on the bottom side and then shingle the avocado on top. Spoon half the pistou over the avocado and top with the vegetables and arugula (rocket). Spoon the rest of the pistou over the arugula and sprinkle with salt and pepper.

Close the sandwich firmly but gently, so all the ingredients meld and stay inside the baguette. Then cut the baguette into 4 sandwiches and enjoy!

I'M RADISH

RADISH

Makes 1 cup

1 teaspoon minced garlic
¾ cup (20 g) tightly packed basil
leaves
½ cup (10 g) tightly packed parsley
leaves
¾ cup (6 fl oz/175 ml) extra-virgin
olive oil
Salt and freshly ground black pepper

Pistou

In a blender, combine the garlic, basil, and parsley. Turn
the blender on medium speed and drizzle in the olive oil.
Season to taste with salt and pepper. Pistou can be kept,
refrigerated, for up to 1 week.

CUCUMBER
I'm cool

flatbread with moroccan chicken meatballs

Kofta, or minced meatballs, with *chermoula*, a vibrant herbal relish, is something I remember from my own childhood and one I love sharing with my daughter. We love cooking the skewers over a real fire, which I feel bonds us together in an almost primal way. Though it's difficult running a restaurant and raising a child, many of my best memories in the kitchen are working side by side with Nur at home.

●

Serves 4

For the chermoula:
1 bunch of mint, stemmed, chopped
1 bunch of cilantro (coriander), chopped
1 teaspoon ground cumin
1 teaspoon sweet paprika
1 teaspoon garlic powder
Pinch of salt
1 teaspoon honey
3½ tablespoons yogurt
2 teaspoons olive oil

For the chicken kofta:
14 oz (400 g) ground (minced) chicken
½ bunch of fresh thyme leaves, chopped
1 tablespoon ground cumin
1 teaspoon ground coriander
Grated zest and juice of 1 lemon
Grated zest and juice of 1 orange

For serving:
2 Flatbreads (recipe follows)
Lettuce
Tomatoes, sliced

Equipment
8 wooden skewers, steeped in water for 30 minutes

Make the chermoula:
In a bowl, stir together the mint, cilantro (coriander), cumin, paprika, garlic powder, salt, honey, yogurt, and olive oil. Serve immediately or refrigerate until needed.

Make the kofta:
In a bowl, mix together the chicken, thyme, cumin, and coriander. Add the lemon juice and orange juice. Then add the zests, mixing well. Shape the meat around the skewers, the shape and thickness of a date but longer, about ¼ cup (50 g) per skewer.

Set up a grill (barbecue) and grill the kebabs over a fire until golden, 4–5 minutes per side. (Alternatively, use a hot well-oiled frying pan for 7–10 minutes.)

For serving:
Warm up the bread on the grill or on the frying pan. Once hot they are ready to serve. Serve the skewers on the bread and add lettuce, some tomatoes, and the chermoula-yogurt mix.

lunch
flatbread with moroccan
chicken meatballs
↓

lunch
garden "fish" finger sticks
↳ p. 58

Makes 30 pieces of flatbread

7⅔ cups (1 kg) all-purpose (plain) flour
3½ tablespoons yogurt
2½ teaspoons (8 g) active dry yeast
1¼ teaspoons salt
Neutral oil

Flatbread

In a stand mixer (or a bowl by hand), combine the flour, 2½ cups (18 fl oz/550 ml) water, yogurt, yeast, and salt and mix well for 15 minutes. (Little hands can chip in here.)

Divide the dough into 1-inch (2.5 cm) balls. Flatten or stretch with your fingers to create a round.

In a frying pan, heat about 2 teaspoons of oil over medium heat. Add a round of dough and once it begins to brown, flip it from side to side to color. Repeat, replenishing the olive oil and allowing to heat each time. Set aside.

MEAT
BALL

FLAT
BREAD

green papaya salad

Serves 2

5 oz (150 g) firm green papaya
2 tablespoons plus 2 teaspoons palm sugar, softened
3 cloves garlic, peeled
2 fresh red bird's eye fresh chilies, halved
4 teaspoons dry-roasted peanuts
½ cup cut snake beans (1¼-inch/ 3 cm lengths)
1 heaping tablespoon good-quality dried shrimp
4 organic cherry or grape tomatoes, halved
4 tablespoons organic fresh lime juice
2 tablespoons plus 2 teaspoons fish sauce

Equipment
Large, deep earthenware mortar and pestle

"

I get slightly annoyed when we are at restaurant and the servers insist on putting the kid's menu in front of the children. I'm aware they mean well, but let's face it, kid's menus are all pretty much the same no matter what end of dining you are in. I think if you, as parents, display enthusiasm for a broad range of good food, kids mimic that behavior and feel confident in trying new things. There are very few foods my kids dislike.

"

One of the ways that I've made sure my kids are interested in food is having them help me with the preparation. This salad, *chat thai som dtum*, or green papaya salad, is perfect for that. It's a truly interactive dish: One kid shreds the green papaya, the other slices the tomatoes and beans. It's easy to make, and gets better with time as the lime and fish sauce permeate the salad. My kids don't mind heat, but if yours do, omit the chili.

•

Using a crimped vegetable peeler peel the outer hard green skin of the papaya off. Lightly shred 4-inch (10 cm) long threads into a bowl of cold water. Rinse the shredded papaya several times, until the water runs clear. Drain and refrigerate.

In a stone mortar and pestle, grind the palm sugar, garlic, and chilies to a rough paste. Add the peanuts, beans, and dried shrimp. Pound until slightly crushed and flattened, being careful not to overpound. Add the tomatoes and gently crush until they just emit juice, keeping them intact. Season with the lime juice and fish sauce.

Using a large metal spoon, mix everything thoroughly until well incorporated and the palm sugar is completely dissolved into the liquid. Add the shredded papaya to the mortar straight out of the refrigerator and use the large metal spoon and pestle to lightly toss and carefully bruise, until the papaya is coated with the juices and the pieces are equally dispersed through the salad.

Scoop the "salad" out of the mortar into a shallow rimmed plate and serve immediately.

⌂ **CHAT THAI (SYDNEY, AUSTRALIA)**

•

☺ **SORAYA, 11; ARTHUR, 10**

<u>lunch</u>
green papaya salad
↓

<u>treats</u>
banana balls
↳ p. 214

adeline grattard

tomato and smoked tofu salad

Serves 4

2 Green Zebra tomatoes, sliced
2 pineapple tomatoes or beefsteak
tomatoes, sliced
Fleur de sel
1 tablespoon olive oil
1 tablespoon toasted sesame oil
1 tablespoon light soy sauce
1 tablespoon fresh lemon juice
1 teaspoon chopped fresh ginger
9 oz (250 g) smoked tofu, cut into
scant ¼-inch (5 mm) dice
½ bunch of basil leaves
½ bunch of mint
1 shallot, finely chopped

During the summer, this is one of our go-to salads. Since I'm rarely off, we tend to make it on a Sunday night and it's become a classic. My kids love it because, among other reasons, it's one of the few times they're allowed to eat with their fingers. I love the depth of flavor contributed by the smoked tofu—which you can make yourself but which we buy from our local Asian market.

Season the tomatoes with a little fleur de sel and set aside.

In a medium bowl, whisk together the olive oil, sesame oil, soy sauce, lemon juice, and ginger. Add the tomatoes, tofu, basil leaves, mint leaves, and shallots and gently toss. Serve immediately.

<u>lunch</u>
tomato and smoked
tofu salad
↓

<u>breakfast</u>
spicy crab omelet
↳ p. 24

andreas caminada

seasonal vegetable salad

Serves 4

For the parsnips and carrots:
2 parsnips, well washed
2 carrots, well washed
2 cups (16 fl oz/475 ml) canola
(rapeseed) oil
10 white peppercorns
1 bay leaf
Salt, to taste

For the chive oil:
1¼ cups (10 fl oz/300 ml) sunflower oil
1 bunch chives, roughly chopped

For the beets and kohlrabi:
3 beets: 1 yellow, 1 red, and 1
Chioggia, peeled and cut into
⅜-inch (1 cm) slices
1 kohlrabi, peeled and cut into
⅜-inch (1 cm) slices
Salt, to taste
2 pinches of powdered (icing) sugar
1 tablespoon white balsamic vinegar
1 tablespoon canola (rapeseed) oil

✻ ◊ 🝙 ✿

CHIVE
FLOWER

The secrets of a good vegetable salad are the different textures and cooking levels of its components. This recipe is intended as an inspiration, not as a binding instruction. The best vegetables are always those that are in season. That is why the salad can look completely different depending on the season. My boys have their own little vegetable and herb garden and their duty is to take good care of the greens that grow there. Whenever things are ripe and ready to eat, we love to pick a nice variety of veggies and make a lovely salad out them. I think giving kids the opportunity to grow vegetable by themselves—even if it's just some small pots with tomato, cucumber, beans, or potato on the balcony—is the best way to make them eat healthy greens with pleasure. It works with Finn and Cla at least!

•

Cook the parsnip and carrots:
Preheat the oven to 175°F (80°C).

Place the parsnips and carrots in a deep pan, cover with the oil, peppercorns, bay leaf, and salt. Cover with foil and confit the vegetables in the oven for 2 hours. Let the vegetables cool in the oil, then quarter them lengthwise.

Make the chive oil:
In a small pan, heat the oil to 140°–158°F (60°–70°C).

Set up a bowl of ice. In a blender, combine the chopped chives and warmed oil and blend. Pass the finished chive oil through a fine-mesh sieve and cool quickly on ice.

Prepare the beets and kohlrabi:
In a bowl, toss the beets and kohlrabi with the salt and sugar and let stand for 5 minutes. Then add the vinegar and oil and let sit until ready to use.

For the vinaigrette:
Generous ⅓ cup (3½ fl oz/100 ml) white balsamic vinegar
2 tablespoons plus 2 teaspoons (20 g) powdered (icing) sugar
1¼ cups (10 fl oz/300 ml) canola (rapeseed) oil
Salt and freshly ground white pepper

For the fennel:
1 bulb fennel, thinly sliced
2 pinches of salt
2 pinches of powdered (icing) sugar
1 tablespoon white balsamic vinegar
1 tablespoon canola (rapeseed) oil

For the garnish (depending on availability):
Fresh and pickled chive flowers
Wild leek flowers
Broccoli flowers
Coriander seeds

<u>Make the vinaigrette:</u>
In a bowl, combine the vinegar and sugar. Work in the oil slowly with a hand blender. Season the vinaigrette with salt and white pepper.

<u>Prepare the fennel:</u>
Shortly before serving, toss together the fennel, salt, sugar, vinegar, and oil.

<u>To serve:</u>
In a frying pan, sauté the parsnips and carrots so the vegetables get a little color.

Place the beets and the kohlrabi in the middle of the plate, then add the sautéed root vegetables on top. Place the sliced fennel on top or next to it. Garnish with a little chive oil, fresh and pickled chive flowers, wild leek flowers, broccoli flowers, and coriander seeds.

andreas caminada

morning glory stir-fried with garlic

Serves 2

7 oz (200 g) morning glory
Juice of 1 lime
1 tablespoon vegetable oil
1 tablespoon minced garlic
1 tablespoon chicken powder or
½ teaspoon salt

We grow morning glory (also called water spinach or *rau muong*), a common Vietnamese green, on our rooftop garden in Da Nang. So whenever we need a quick lunch, Arya heads to the roof to go pick some. Like most kids, she doesn't eat that many vegetables, but she's been eating this, stir-fried with garlic, since she was a baby. When she was younger, I'd just give her the leaves, cut up. Now I use both the stem and the leaf. It's the only vegetable dish that my daughter is passionate about and requests daily. Morning glory can be replaced with other leafy vegetables such as bok choy or spinach.

•

Cut the morning glory into pieces 6 inches (15 cm) long. Rinse and then soak in water for 10 minutes with a bit of lime juice.

Heat a frying pan over high heat. Add the vegetable oil. When the oil is hot, add the garlic and fry until golden. Add the morning glory and stir-fry for 2 minutes. Add the chicken powder, toss, and transfer to a serving dish.

ALIASES:
WATER SPINACH
ONG CHOY
KANG-KUNG

lunch

⌂ NÉN RESTAURANT
(DA NANG, VIETNAM)
•
☺ **ARYA, 5**

<u>lunch</u>
morning glory stir-fried
with garlic
↓

<u>dinner</u>
lemongrass clams
↳ p. 160

cracked green wheat chicken soup

Serves 4–6

For the spiced chicken stock:
2 tablespoons olive oil or ghee
1 whole chicken (about 4½ lb/2 kg)
or 4 chicken legs
1 medium onion, diced
4 cloves garlic, diced
10–12 black peppercorns
½ teaspoon cracked cardamom pods
½ teaspoon fennel seeds
2 tablespoons salt
2 teaspoons Lebanese 7-spice mix
1 bay leaf

For the shorbat freekeh:
3 tablespoons olive oil or ghee
1 medium onion, diced
2 cloves garlic, minced
½ teaspoon ground coriander
½ teaspoon ground cumin
1 cup (180 g) freekeh

For the garnish:
1 lemon
¼ cup fresh parsley, stemmed

"
My child grew up in the restaurant,
so Zain eats what I cook. I'm lucky
because my child's an adventurous
one when it comes to eating.
We sing Daniel Tiger's *Try a New
Food, It Might Taste Good!* Every
once in a while, Zain obliges.
"

Cracked green wheat chicken soup, or *shorbat freekeh*, was one of my favorite comfort foods growing up. Every culture has a version of chicken soup. What makes this particular soup unique, beyond the warming spices of the chicken stock, is the freekeh, a durum wheat that gets its smoky flavor from being fire-roasted in its early stages (hence the term green wheat). I have vivid memories of this hot soup made at my grandmother's house in Southern California, where freekeh was more readily available. I really started to love the chewiness of freekeh, which adds great thickness to a soup, turning it into a savory porridge. The soup reminds me of *arroz caldo* (page 126), a dish my Filipino husband grew up with, a thick and aromatic rice porridge that is super comforting especially when you're sick.

•

Make the spiced chicken stock:

In a stockpot, heat the olive oil over medium heat. Add the chicken to the pot, skin-side down, and give it a good sear for 3–5 minutes to give it a nice brown color all over.

Toss the onion and garlic into the pot and sauté until translucent. Add the peppercorns, cardamom, and fennel and sauté until you can smell the spices. At this point, the oil's been infused with the chicken fat.

Add 12 cups (3 quarts/liters) water to the pot, enough to cover the chicken. Add the salt, 7-spice mix, and bay leaf and mix until thoroughly incorporated. Bring to a boil over medium heat, then reduce the heat to a simmer and cook for 1½–2 hours, depending on the size and type of chicken. Skim off any scum that rises to the top if needed. Pull out the chicken to cool. Strain the broth and adjust the seasoning.

When cool enough to handle, break and pull apart the chicken into shreds. Measure out half of the chicken for this

🏠 REEM'S (OAKLAND,
SAN FRANCISCO,
CALIFORNIA, US)
•
☺ ZAIN, 2

lunch
cracked green wheat
chicken soup
↓

breakfast
za'atar egg
salad sandwich
⮡ p. 22

dish and save the remainder for another dish. You can discard the carcass and fry the chicken skin for garnish.

Set aside 8 cups (2 quarts/liters) of stock for this dish and freeze the remainder. Stock can be kept frozen up to 3 months.

Make the shorbat freekeh:
In a large saucepan, heat the oil over medium heat. Add the onion and sauté until translucent, 2–3 minutes. Add the garlic, coriander, and cumin. As soon as you smell the spices, add the freekeh. Mix thoroughly until every grain of freekeh is coated with the oil.

Add the stock and bring to a boil. Then reduce to a simmer and cook for 45 minutes to 1 hour to reduce the stock by half. Stir in the shredded chicken.

To plate, divide into four bowls and top with a squeeze of lemon and fresh parsley.

reem assil

karena armstrong

lunch box noodle bowl

We have three boys, five years apart in total, so it's safe to say our house is hectic. The boys are a hurricane of energy and, especially as they get ready for school, the mornings pass in a blur. But they still need to eat. Each of the kids plays sports after school, so they need a healthy and filling lunch. For these, I prepare all the ingredients the night before, sometimes at the beginning of the week, and simply assemble in that morning rush.

•

Makes 8 lunch boxes

For the noodles:
5 oz (150 g) baby spinach
17½ oz (500 g) noodles, such as sweet potato noodles/soba/udon
1 oz (30 g) fresh ginger
6 tablespoons soy sauce
2 tablespoons plus 2 teaspoons extra-virgin olive oil
2 teaspoons toasted sesame oil

For the tofu:
3½ tablespoons rice bran oil or similar neutral oil
17½ oz (500 g) firm tofu, cut into 8 even slices
2 tablespoons plus 2 teaspoons soy sauce
2 tablespoons plus 2 teaspoons oyster sauce or hoisin sauce
2 tablespoons fresh lemon juice
2 teaspoons toasted sesame oil

For the garnishes:
3 bunches Chinese broccoli or similar greens
3 sheets nori
⅓ cup (50 g) toasted sesame seeds
7 oz (200 g) frozen shelled edamame, thawed
2 avocados
4 free-range eggs, hard-boiled (for 6 minutes)

Cook the noodles:

Put the spinach in a colander and set in the sink. Cook the noodles according to the package directions. Drain the hot noodles into the colander over the spinach and mix well. Finely grate the ginger into a large container and add to the noodles. Add the soy sauce, olive oil, and sesame oil and mix really well. Refrigerate until required.

Make the tofu:

Heat a large frying pan over medium-high heat. Add the oil to the pan and when hot, add the tofu and cook both sides until golden brown. Remove to a plate. In a bowl or cup, whisk together the soy sauce, oyster sauce, lemon juice, and sesame oil. Pour over the hot tofu. Cool until needed.

Prepare the garnishes:

Set up an ice bath. Steam the Chinese broccoli very quickly and plunge into the ice bath to chill. Drain well and chop into small bits. Toast the nori in a low oven until crisp. Store in a sealed container.

Have all the ingredients ready to assemble the lunch boxes, but don't slice the avocados or peel the eggs until the day of. Use the extra dressing from the tofu and noodles to add moisture.

⌂ **THE SALOPIAN INN (MCLAREN VALE, AUSTRALIA)**

•

☺ **HARRY, 14; SEBASTIAN, 12; FLETCHER, 10**

<u>lunch</u>
lunch box noodle bowl

↓

<u>dinner</u>
roasted lamb shoulder, bao, and pickles

↳ p. 176

spiced potatoes with peas

Serves 4–6

1 tablespoon vegetable oil
½ teaspoon cumin seeds
5 dried red chilies
17½ oz (500 g) white potatoes (not baking or new potatoes), unpeeled and boiled
1 teaspoon ground turmeric
7 oz (200 g) frozen peas
1 teaspoon salt

❀ ◊ 🜂 ❧

"

In the early years of setting up my restaurant, I only saw my children asleep when I returned from work. I often left before they got up for school. I did not cook for the family at all in the first year after opening the restaurant. I would take food from the restaurant back home and leave it in the fridge for my husband and my older son to eat. My younger son was mainly living on food prepared by my older son. After the first year, I started coming home in between service and would cook for my children, and serve them supper before going back to the restaurant. This is the pattern that has gone on for the last two years. There are of course times when I cannot go back home and the children are very happy to order takeaway on that day!

"

Aloo mattar sabzi, a classic combination of peas (*mattar*) and potatoes (*aloo*) simmered in sauce (*sabzi*) has always been a favorite. When my sons were younger, I weaned them both on bowls of boiled peas. (Though Fariz would frequently squish them without eating any.) These days, both boys love the combination in this *sabzi*. One prefers it with rice, the other with *paratha* or *puri*, and me with thickly buttered toast. For children for whom spice is new, the familiarity of peas helps ease them into the world of new flavors.

•

In a large cast-iron skillet, heat the oil over high heat. Add the cumin seeds and chilies and immediately reduce the heat, as you do not want the seeds and chilies to burn. Roughly break the potatoes into lumps and add to the pan. Add the turmeric. Stir the potatoes and spices for a couple minutes. Add the frozen peas and salt followed by 2 cups (16 fl oz/475 ml) warm water. Cook the potatoes over high heat until there is a glossy shine on the potatoes, about 5 minutes longer. The texture should not be dry—this is a thick potato and peas dish meant to be scooped up and eaten with bread.

<u>lunch</u>
spiced potatoes
with peas
↓

<u>breakfast</u>
spicy scrambled eggs
↳ p. 14

jonny rhodes

chili mac and cheese

Serves 4

Salt
3 cups (255 g) large elbow macaroni
1 tablespoon olive oil
1 cup (160 g) diced yellow onion
1 lb (455 g) ground (minced) beef
Freshly ground black pepper
½ cup (130 g) tomato paste (purée)
½ cup (130 g) pepper paste
1 cup (8 fl oz/250 ml) milk
1 stick (4 oz/113 g) unsalted butter
2 cups (225 g) shredded white
Cheddar cheese

As I am from Texas and live in Texas, I can tell you that chili is life. Mac and cheese is also life. In this dish, I bring the two together. There's a little bit of a kick in this, thanks to the pepper paste, but my kids love the heat. It's a part of their lives. At Indigo, I really had time only to cook breakfast with the kids, but I'd also make a pot of this for Athena to take to school. In an airtight container, it keeps well and hot until lunchtime.

•

In a large pot of salted boiling water, cook the macaroni until al dente according to the package directions. Drain well.

Meanwhile, in a large frying pan, heat the olive oil over medium heat until shimmering. Add the onions and cook until tender but not burnt, about 5 minutes. Add the beef, season with salt and pepper, and cook until browned and crumbled, 10–12 minutes. Carefully drain off the fat from the pan.

Return the beef to low heat, stir in the tomato paste (purée) and pepper paste and cook for another 5–8 minutes, to allow the flavors to commingle. Add the milk, butter, and Cheddar and bring to a boil. Add the drained macaroni. Serve as soon as the ingredients are well melted.

<u>lunch</u>
chili mac and cheese
↓

<u>dinner</u>
smoked sweet
potato gnocchi
↳ p. 152

kasha varnishkes

Serves 4

12 oz (340 g) fresh pasta sheets (or
8 oz/225 g dried farfalle pasta)
Kosher salt
⅔ cup (115 g) buckwheat groats
10 tablespoons (140 g) butter, divided
¼ cup (7 g) minced fresh dill
9 oz (250 g) yellow onion, small diced
½ cup (115 g) finely chopped pitted
prunes

Kasha varnishkes, a traditional Ashkenazi dish made with buckwheat groats (kasha) and bowtie noodles (varnishkes in Yiddish), is one of the few things I can get both kids to gobble up without any pushback. It's a way to introduce a challenging but incredibly nutritious grain to young eaters by mixing it with more approachable bowtie pasta. Also, it's one of those recipes for which I usually have everything I need on hand, so it's perfect when I haven't had time to stop by the grocery store in a bit. As for kasha, also called buckwheat groats, I highly recommend seeking out good, imported buckwheat groats from an Eastern European grocer.

•

To make the bowties:

Cut the fresh pasta sheets into 2-inch (5 cm) squares. Accordion fold each square 3–4 bends. Crimp the center of each accordion to form a bow shape. Use a blunt tool, like the butt of a butter knife or a dowel, to help crimp each bow if the dough seems dry. This should yield about 100 bow ties. Place the finished bowties in a large, covered container, being careful not to smash them. Refrigerate. Bowties can be made up to 24 hours in advance.

To cook the bowties:

Pour 1⅓ cups (10½ fl oz/325 ml) water into a 1-quart (1-liter) saucepan. Season the water generously with salt. Add the buckwheat and bring to a boil over high heat. Reduce the heat and gently simmer, covered with a tight-fitting lid. Simmer until the water is absorbed and the groats are fully cooked, about 15 minutes. Set aside. Buckwheat can be cooked up to 4 days in advance. Transfer the cooked buckwheat to a lidded storage container and refrigerate if making in advance.

KASHA
VARNISHKES

dinner
raclette dinner with
red wine–pickled onions
↳ p. 136

To finish and assemble:
Fill a large pot with heavily salted water and bring to a rolling boil. While waiting for the water to come up, place half the butter, dill, and a pinch of salt in a large mixing bowl and set aside. Place the other half of the butter in a sauté pan over medium heat. When the butter is foaming, add the diced onions. Sauté, stirring regularly, until the onions are fully cooked and golden to dark brown, but not burnt. Getting a good amount of color in the onions is critical for flavor in the final dish. This should be a quick, somewhat uneven cook, about 10 minutes. Add the reserved buckwheat and the prunes to the onions and continue to cook until the buckwheat is hot and well mixed with the onions. This will take a little longer and might require a lid to steam the buckwheat if reheating from the refrigerator. Make sure that the prunes are evenly distributed and not clumped together.

When the pasta water has come to a rapid boil, place the bowties in the water and cook for just a couple minutes, until the pasta is fully cooked. If using dry farfalle pasta, it will take more like 8–10 minutes to fully cook. When the pasta is done, use a spider to transfer it to the prepared bowl with the butter, prunes, dill, and salt, giving the pasta a good shake to remove excess water. Immediately start tossing the contents of the bowl vigorously to make an emulsion with the butter and the wet pasta. If you let the bowl sit before tossing, the butter will melt and not cling to the pasta properly. Once the contents have been mixed together and all the butter is melted, add the buckwheat, prune, and onion mixture to the pasta and toss to mix evenly.

Serve immediately.

jp mcmahon

pasta with butter and parmesan

This dish perfectly encapsulates my kids: simple eaters who love bold flavors. It also demonstrates our love of Italian food here in Ireland. Though it may seem like a simple dish to make, there are a few things that take it to the next level. First, I add my own reduced chicken stock, which gives the dish a lot of body and umami. Second, I don't skimp on the butter. That's the whole point of the dish. Third, buy really good Parmesan or a local equivalent. The quality of the cheese is paramount. Last, you can try and make your own pasta. We don't do this a lot, but there is something amazing about showing your kids how to make fresh pasta. Dump flour and eggs on the table and make as much mess as possible.

Serves 4

For the pasta dough:
4 cups (500 g) tipo "00" flour
5 eggs or 10 egg yolks, lightly whisked

For assembly:
8 cups (2 quarts/liters) homemade chicken stock
Sea salt
7 tablespoons (100 g) butter, cubed
Generous ¾ cup (50 g) freshly grated Parmesan cheese

"
I encourage my kids to be adventurous eaters in two ways: First, by trying to get them to try small bits of whatever food I'm eating (from sushi to seaweed). Second (perhaps more controversially), by giving them a euro when they eat something new. This might seem preposterous, and I once handed over nearly €30 (when we were on holiday in Spain), but my daughter did try thirty new foods and discovered she loved mussels. Thankfully, I don't need to do it too often now!
"

•

Make the pasta dough:

Place the flour in a bowl and make a well in the center. Add the whisked eggs to the center and combine with your fingers. Transfer the dough to a work surface. Flour your hands and knead until silky smooth. Cover and rest in the refrigerator for 30 minutes before rolling.

Roll the pasta by hand, or with a machine, until you have reached the desired thinness. Cut the pasta and allow to hang or dust with flour before cooking.

To assemble:

In a pot, cook the chicken stock over medium heat until reduced to a generous ¾ cup (7 fl oz/200 ml), about 1 hour.

In a large pot of salted boiling water, cook the pasta until al dente. Reserving about ¼ cup (2 fl oz/60 ml) of the cooking water, drain the pasta and return to the pot. Add the reduced chicken stock, pasta cooking water, and butter and mix until thoroughly combined. Season to taste with salt.

Serve garnished with the freshly grated Parmesan.

lunch

<u>lunch</u>
pasta with butter
and parmesan
↓

<u>dinner</u>
whole baked turbot
with mussels
and buttered greens
↳ p. 182

vladimir mukhin

zucchini pancakes with guacamole

Serves 4

For the zucchini pancakes:
½ cup (60 g) all-purpose (plain) flour, sifted
1¼ teaspoons (5 g) granulated sugar
Scant ½ teaspoon (2 g) baking soda (bicarbonate of soda)
Scant ½ teaspoon (2 g) baking powder
Scant ½ teaspoon salt
1 oz (36 g) fresh spinach, chopped
1 egg
6 tablespoons (3 fl oz/90 ml) whole milk
4 oz (110 g) zucchini (courgettes), peeled and grated

For the guacamole:
1 (100 g) avocado
4 teaspoons (12 g) finely chopped chili pepper
4 teaspoons (12 g) fresh cilantro (coriander) leaves
4 teaspoons (20 ml) extra-virgin olive oil
1 teaspoon (4 ml) fresh lime juice
1 teaspoon salt

For assembly:
5½ tablespoons (2¾ fl oz/80 ml) sunflower oil
2 tablespoons (4 g) dill, chopped
1 oz (30 g) kale, washed, dried, and roughly chopped
2 oz (60 g) fresh green peas

My daughter loves zucchini (courgettes). When she was very little, she collected some leftover change, saving it until she had a little pile of coins. I was surprised. My daughter is a princess and has everything she needs. But she showed me her savings and told me, "Daddy, I want to buy zucchini." So that Sunday, my sacred no-work day, we headed to our favorite farmers' market, Danilovskiy Rynok. I taught her how to pick out the best produce, and then we came home and made these *oladyi*, something between a pancake and fritter. Since then, they've become a staple in our home and we've even put them on the menu at both White Rabbit and Gorynich, where they've become bestsellers.

•

Make the zucchini pancakes:
In a large bowl, mix together the flour, sugar, baking soda (bicarb), baking powder, salt, spinach, egg, and milk. Add the grated zucchini (courgettes) and stir. Set aside for 10 minutes.

Make the guacamole:
Blend the avocado into a purée. Add the chili, cilantro (coriander), olive oil, lime juice, and salt. Blend again until smooth.

To assemble:
In a frying pan, heat the oil over medium heat until shimmering-hot. Add the batter by ¼ cup (2 fl oz/60 ml) and fry the pancakes on both sides until evenly cooked.

Serve the pancakes sprinkled with dill, guacamole, green peas, and kale on the side.

"

Since both my children were very little, my wife and I have always tried to use the freshest and most diverse products for them to eat at home. We believe that good eating habits start in the family. My kids always have good fruits and vegetables at hand. My wife is vegetarian, so we all eat a lot of greens and, you know, children copy their parents. So we need to give them a good example. Sunday is my family day, I never work on this day and together with my kids—first my daughter, but now together with my son as well—we have our ritual. We go to our nearby market, we choose the products, we try different foods. We don't forbid them to eat fast food since we don't want to make it a forbidden fruit. But my kids just know from their experience that energy comes from good and healthy food, that's it.

"

yoshihiro
narisawa

chicken yakitori

⅓ cup plus 1 tablespoon (100 ml)
white wine
⅓ cup plus 1 tablespoon (100 ml)
soy sauce
1 teaspoon (15 g) honey
2 boneless, skinless chicken thighs
⅓ cup plus 1 tablespoon (100 ml) sake
⅓ cup plus 1 tablespoon (100 ml) mirin
1 tablespoon cornstarch (cornflour)
2 eggplants (aubergines), each cut
into eighths
1 green bell pepper, cut into eighths
1 leek, cut into eighths lengthwise

"

It's not easy to make time to cook at
home, but I think it's also important
to let my family visit the kitchen of
the restaurant often, to show them
how I cook in the kitchen and to give
them the opportunity to dine there.
Whenever I can cook at home on my
days off, I make time to cook together
with my family as often as I can.

"

When my kids were growing up—and still today—we ate
a lot of chicken. It's a high-protein, low-cost food you
can get at any time. Yakitori is a simple, quick way to prepare
it. Traditionally served on skewers, I find it works just as
well without. The most appealing part, my kids tell me, is
the delicious salty soy sauce with the additional sweetness,
thanks to honey. After a quick marinade, the chicken is ready
to go in a matter of minutes and there are never any leftovers.

In a small saucepan, bring the white wine to a boil over
medium heat to cook off the alcohol. Reduce the heat and
stir in the soy sauce and honey until dissolved. Remove
from the heat and let cool.

Once cool, add the chicken to the liquid and marinate for
15 minutes. Remove the chicken from the marinade (reserve
the marinade) and pat the chicken dry.

In a large frying pan, cook the chicken thighs over medium-
high heat until cook through, about 6 minutes per side.

In a bowl, stir together the reserved marinade, sake, mirin,
and cornstarch (cornflour). Add to the pan and cook until
the sauce is thickened. Add the eggplants (aubergines),
bell pepper, and leek and cook until the vegetables have
softened and gained color, approximately 7 minutes.

For serving, plate the chicken and vegetables together, with
the sauce poured on top.

🏠 **NARISAWA**
(TOKYO, JAPAN)
•
☺ **LEO, 20; NOA, 17**

<u>lunch</u>
chicken yakitori
↓

<u>dinner</u>
miso-marinated cod
↳ p. 164

o

FORMER EGG   FUTURE CHICKEN

lemony chicken with insima

Serves 4

For the chicken:
14 oz (400 g) skinless, boneless chicken breasts, cut into medium chunks
1½ teaspoons (3 g) chicken seasoning
1½ teaspoons (3 g) cayenne pepper
Salt and freshly ground black pepper
5 teaspoons (5 g) dried mixed herbs
2½ tablespoons extra-virgin olive oil
½ onion, diced
2 large cloves garlic, finely minced
3–4 medium Peppadew peppers, stemmed and halved
7 oz (200 g) chomolia or kale, deribbed and cut into strips
1 teaspoon (3 g) paprika
1 tablespoon honey
Juice of 1 large lemon

For the pap:
6 cups (800 g) maize meal, also called mealie-meal

For the garnish:
Dried pumpkin flowers or micro herbs

Insima, also called *pap*, is a staple made from maize that the majority of South Africans, and thus my own boys, grew up eating. Though originally it was made with sorghum flour, after it was introduced in the sixteenth century, maize soon became the common grain. Sandiso, my eldest son, who is studying to be a lawyer, loves this dish and often helps me make it for an easy lunch on break from university. It's quick to prepare and is a great way to incorporate vegetables—here *chomolia*, also called African kale, though most kales will do.

Cook the chicken:
Season the chicken well with the chicken seasoning, cayenne, black pepper, and some of the mixed herb.

In a large wok, lightly fry the chicken breasts over medium heat. Remove from the heat just before the chicken is ready.

In a separate frying pan, heat the olive oil over medium heat. Add the onion, garlic, peppers and the remaining dried mixed herbs and cook until the onions are translucent, about 7 minutes. Stir the onions into the wok with the chicken. Once well mixed, stir in the kale and cook until the kale has softened, 2–3 minutes. Be careful not to overcook the kale.

Add the paprika, honey, and lemon juice to the mix. Stir the mixture, making sure there is balance between the sweet and the sour. Season with salt and black pepper.

Make the pap:
In a bowl, combine 3⅓ cups (440 g) of the maize meal with a scant 2 cups (15 fl oz/450 ml) cold water.

In a pot, bring ¾ cup plus 1 tablespoon (7 fl oz/200 ml) water to a boil. Reduce to a simmer and stir in the maize mixture. Stir constantly to prevent the mixture from setting at the

🏠 **KUMYOLI CULINARY EXPERIENCES (JOHANNESBURG, SOUTH AFRICA)**
•
☺ **SANDISO, 23; BHONGO, 16**

lunch
lemony chicken
with insima
↓

dinner
butter shrimp
and taro wedges
↳ p. 162

bottom of the pot. Once well mixed, simmer for 15 minutes, until the mixture has a porridge-like consistency.

Carefully, stir the remaining 2⅔ cups (360 g) maize meal into the simmering porridge. Once added, stir briskly, in a single direction, using a wooden spoon in a folding motion from the bottom up to the sides to prevent lumps. Continue stirring constantly until the mixture becomes thicker. Mix well, then cover, reduce the heat, and cook another 10 minutes.

To serve:
Fill a ramekin with pap, allowing it to take the shape of the ramekin. Turn the ramekin out onto a plate and serve with the lemony chicken, garnished with pumpkin flowers or micro herbs.

daniel rose and marie-aude rose

calf's liver "au vinaigre" with sautéed brussels sprouts and bacon

Serves 4

1 lb (455 g) Brussels sprouts
1 tablespoon olive oil
4 oz (115 g) bacon, chopped
4 thin slices calf's liver (about 4 oz/
115 g each)
1 teaspoon fine sea salt
Freshly ground white pepper
½ cup (65 g) all-purpose (plain) flour
4 tablespoons (60 g) unsalted butter
1 onion, thinly sliced
½ cup (4 fl oz/120 ml) raspberry
vinegar or red wine vinegar
½ cup (4 fl oz/120 ml) crème fraîche
(if you can't find crème fraîche, use
heavy cream; don't use sour cream)

Willie and Otto have always eaten what we eat and we all eat together. They might push some around or eat less of it, but we've never made anything special for them in that sense. They've each developed their own distinct taste. Willie, our daughter, hates cheeseburgers, but this hearty calf's liver dish is one of her favorites. It's not something to pig out on, nor do I [Daniel] think that that should be the metric of success.

•

Trim the stem ends of the Brussels sprouts and remove a few of the outer leaves. Cut them in half through the stem.

In a large frying pan, heat the olive oil over medium-high heat. Add the bacon and start to cook. Add the Brussels sprouts, cut-sides down, and allow them to color on that side, about 3 minutes. Add ½ cup (4 fl oz/120 ml) water, cover, and cook for 10 minutes, until the Brussels sprouts are tender.

Season the liver slices on both sides with the salt and pepper to taste, then dredge them in the flour. Tap to remove excess flour.

In each of 2 large frying pans, melt 2 tablespoons (30 g) of the butter over medium heat. Add 2 slices of liver to each pan and cook 2 minutes on each side, giving them a nice color. Set aside and keep warm.

In these same pans, cook the sliced onion, allowing it to soften but not color, for about 2 minutes. Add the vinegar and let it reduce almost all the way, then stir in the crème fraîche.

Serve the liver on a nice oval dish with the sauce poured over them and the Brussels sprouts on the side.

⌂ **CHEZ LA VIEILLE (PARIS, FRANCE), LE COUCOU, LA MERCERIE (NEW YORK, NEW YORK, US)**
•
☺ **WILHELMINA, 8; OTTO, 6**

lunch
calf's liver "au vinaigre" with sautéed brussels sprouts and bacon
↓

breakfast
country cheese with blueberries and cream
↳ p. 46

baked fish and rice

Serves 2

2–3 oz (80–100 g) skin-on white
fish fillet, such as snapper, grouper,
barramundi
1½ teaspoons fish sauce
A tiny pinch of white pepper
1 clove garlic, peeled
½ teaspoon salt
½ teaspoon neutral oil
1 tablespoon thinly sliced shallot
1½ tablespoons diced blanched
young pumpkin
1½ tablespoons diced blanched ivy
gourd
1½ tablespoons snake beans, cut
in half
1 okra, thinly sliced
1 tablespoon corn kernels
1–2 tablespoons soy sauce
¾ cup (120 g) cooked rice
½ cup (4 fl oz/120 ml) chicken stock
1 organic egg

The first two or three years after our son Dtaychiit was born,
he spent a lot of time in the restaurant. Whatever we had in
the fridges, he'd eat; and since we've always cooked with a lot
of vegetables at Bo.lan, it was a natural fit. We'd just throw
in whatever veggies we were making for service. For us, as
a family, it was great since it did double duty: We wanted to
encourage him to eat more vegetables and we wanted him
to be able to feed himself without being spoon fed, which
neither of us could do during service. The dish called *khao op*
(*khao* meaning "rice" and *op* meaning "baked") was so popular
that now it's on the Bo.lan children's menu, named, naturally,
after Dtaychiit, as Khao Op Dtaychiit.

Marinate the fish in the fish sauce and white pepper for
10 minutes.

Heat a heavy-bottomed saucepan over medium heat.
Once hot, add the fish skin-side down and cook until crispy,
5–7 minutes. Flip and continue cooking for an additional
5–7 minutes. Remove from the heat and let rest.

Meanwhile, pound the garlic and salt in a mortar and pestle.

Add the oil to the saucepan and heat over medium heat until
shimmering. Add the shallot and pounded garlic. Cook until
fragrant, about 3 minutes. Add the remaining vegetables and
allow to caramelize, about 3 minutes. Add the soy sauce,
agitating for 30 seconds. Add the cooked rice and stir-fry
for about 30 seconds. Add the stock and bring to a boil.
Once boiling, crack the egg on top of the rice, cover the pan,
reduce the heat, and cook gently for 4–7 minutes.

To serve, gently spoon into a bowl and place the grilled fish
on top.

SNAPPER

lunch

🏠 **BO.LAN (BANGKOK, THAILAND)**
•
☺ **DTAYCHIIT KEITH, 8; DAYCHATHORN ETHAN, 5**

<u>lunch</u>
baked fish and rice
↓

<u>snacks</u>
spring rolls
↳ p. 108

duangporn "bo" songvisava and dylan jones

pork and beans with orzo

Serves 6

For the pork:
1 tablespoon black peppercorns
2 bay leaves
2 sprigs fresh thyme
3 tablespoons coarse salt
Canola (rapeseed) oil
5½ lb (2.5 kg) pork belly

For the beans:
2 tablespoons olive oil
3 medium red onions, coarsely chopped
3 cloves garlic, crushed
3 cups (24 fl oz/710 ml) tomato purée (passata)
2 cups (16 fl oz/475 ml) concentrated chicken stock
2 cans (16 oz/450 g) borlotti beans, drained
2 cans (16 oz/450 g) red kidney beans, drained
2 cans (16 oz/450 g) white beans, drained
Dried oregano
Smoked paprika
Salt and freshly ground black pepper
7 oz (200 g) Cheddar or mozzarella cheese, cubed

For the orzo:
Salt
3⅓ cups (500 g) orzo pasta
3 tablespoons basil pesto

Pork and beans are an old-school combination that I remember eating growing up in Franschhoek. It's a hearty dish that heats up your body when you need it, nourishes when you've worked hard, and satisfies when you are really hungry. I always have beans in the pantry somewhere— borlotti, sugar beans, red kidney beans—and here they really come in handy. The orzo, meanwhile, rounds out the meal, a perfect Sunday lunch that spreads to Monday lunch, too.

•

Prepare the pork:
Preheat the oven to 480°F (250°C/Gas Mark 9).

Crush the peppercorns, bay leaves, and thyme with the coarse salt and a drizzle of canola oil. Using a sharp knife, score the skin of the pork belly and rub the aromatic mixture all over the pork.

Place in a roasting pan, fat-side up, and roast for 15 minutes. Reduce the oven temperature to 350°F (180°C/Gas Mark 4) and roast for another 1 hour 20 minutes. Remove from the oven and place a sheet pan on top of the meat, with enough weight to press down on the belly very lightly. Allow to cool like this for 2–3 hours. (This process is optional, but I like to have the fat side fairly flat, and you also get rid of the excess fat.) Chop the cooled meat into cubes.

Make the beans:
Add the olive oil to a wide pan and slowly sweat the onions and garlic in it, without allowing them to brown, about 4 minutes.

lunch

<u>lunch</u>
pork and beans
with orzo
↓

<u>breakfast</u>
herbed mascarpone
scrambled eggs
↳ p. 16

Add the tomato purée (passata), chicken stock, and herbs and bring quickly to a simmer, and then cook slowly for 10 minutes, or until the sauce starts to thicken. Stir in the beans. When they're heated through, add the cubed pork and cook for 8 minutes. Check for seasoning and pull off the heat, then add the cubes of cheddar to allow it to melt slowly into the sauce.

<u>To assemble:</u>
Cook the orzo in boiling salted water until al dente.
Drain and toss the pasta with the pesto. Serve alongside the pork and beans.

500 grams of
ORZO (or so)

*

A snack is as a snack does. Most snacks, depending on timing and serving size, can easily become lunches, dinners, or sides. Many lunches, dinners, and treats, meanwhile, can pinch-hit as snacks, depending on the portion size. Nevertheless, they are to the parents' kitchen repertoire what Dad jokes are to Dad and hugs are to Mom: absolutely necessary for the well-being of the household.

Yet as a genre, snacks strike terror into the heart of parents everywhere, especially afternoon snacks, during the no-man's-land between lunch and dinner. This is treacherous terrain for us parents, this long stretch of time lacking in formal mealtime. Hold out too long, meltdowns ensue or else, worse, that old chestnut "You'll spoil your appetite!" actually does comes true. Small is the window to sate your child without prejudicing his or her appetite for dinner.

Timing isn't the only challenge. For parents, the preparation of snacks can seem a Herculean task. It's already enough to prepare three meals a day. Snacks can be the straws that break the camel's back. Into this parental void, a glut of prepackaged snack foods has happily galumphed. Not to pooh-pooh these solutions—for many indeed are both delicious and nutritious —but by and large, homemade is better.

The trick is, as always, how to find the time. The recipes that follow consist of two approaches: Some of them solve by minimizing the labor and optimizing the prep to fit a convenient schedule. Food that can be made ahead of time with no fuss whatsoever is good snack food. Such are the strengths of Manoella Buffara's Zucchini Bread (page 122) or Jeremy Charles's Parsnip and Apple Soup (page 114). Ana Roš's Frico (page 130) is a free-form mash-up, made à la minute in a few minutes' time. Another approach is to turn snacks, and their preparation, into the rhythm-and-flow of the afternoon activity. So it is that Rye and his mom, Lee Anne Wong, stuff dumplings together (page 116) or Dtaychiit and his brother, Daychathorn, help their parents fold spring rolls (page 108). Snacks, and their preparation, become content for the afternoon.

A note about size. All food, at some point, becomes bite-size. But snacks are best when they are endemically so. Thus dumplings and spring rolls, slices of bread, and things on crackers are perfect snacks. They're made to grab for sustenance without breaking the rhythm of activity, and they're small and quick enough to leave afternoons and appetites intact.

*

snacks

kabocha squash with oats and apples

Serves 2

For the kabocha squash purée:
1 medium kabocha squash (Japanese pumpkin), peeled, seeded, and diced
2 tablespoons brown butter
1 cup (8 fl oz/240 ml) vegetable stock
2 tablespoons golden raisins (sultanas)
Salt and freshly ground black pepper

For the oats:
1 cup (80 g) organic rolled oats

For finishing:
1 Honeycrisp apple, peeled and medium diced, for garnish

Equipment
Pressure cooker

I want Leo to grow up tasting the heirloom varietals I love so much. I hope those sacred flavors, etched into his memory, inspire him to take care of my Southern seed bank he will inherit from me. So every day we try and make sure Leo tries something new. He always surprises me with the things that he likes and doesn't like. For his first taste of real food I made several varieties of heirloom squash. I was so excited for him to taste them. But, as it turns out, he hated it. He spit the squash right out and started gagging. It was one of the most humbling moments of my career. Thankfully, after a lot of experimentation, we settled on this recipe, which uses kabocha squash but rounded out with oats and a crisp apple.

•

Make the kabocha squash purée:
In a pressure cooker, combine the squash (pumpkin), brown butter, stock, raisins (sultanas), and salt and pepper to taste. Seal and cook at high pressure for 7 minutes. Transfer the ingredients to a blender (open the blender cap steam vent) and purée until smooth.

For the oats:
Meanwhile, in a saucepan, bring 2 cups (16 fl oz/475 ml) water to a boil. Add the oats and stir until there are no clumps. Reduce the heat to low and cook for 15–20 minutes.

To finish:
Stir the squash purée into the oats, then garnish with the apple over the top.

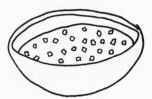

⌂ **AUDREY (NASHVILLE, TENNESSEE, US)**
•
☺ **LEO, 1**

<u>snacks</u>
kabocha squash
with oats and apples
↓

<u>breakfast</u>
japanese omelet
with cheddar and formula
↳ p. 18

mamey shake

Makes 2 shakes

1½ cups (12 fl oz/350 ml) oat milk
or almond milk
4¼ oz (120 g) mamey pulp (or
persimmon)
¼ teaspoon (5 g) grated pixtle*
¼ vanilla bean (or 1 teaspoon vanilla
extract)
2 tablespoons (10 g) amaranth grain
3 ice cubes (85 g)

"

We have a very clear rule: 'Try it.'
When we eat out, whether it's at a
market, street food or a restaurant,
I like them to taste several dishes so
we share. Our rule is that they should
try at least a little bit. If they don't like
it, it's okay. But they should always
try it. This simple rule has made them
very adventurous eaters.

"

In Mexico, we tend to have a late and heavy lunch, so often
Lea and Julieta have this simple nutritious smoothie for
dinner. But it also makes a wonderful snack. Amaranth, an
ancient grain grown since pre-Hispanic times, is gluten-free
and high in protein and in fiber. And mamey is a tropical fruit
I often use in my restaurants, not only for its flavor but for
the creamy consistency and beautiful orange color. After
blending, I add some grated *pixtle*, as the pits (stones) of the
mamey are called, to give a pleasing bitter almond flavor.
And while you could use regular milk, I prefer nondairy
versions like oat, coconut, or almond milks.

•

In a high-powered blender, combine the oat milk, mamey
pulp, pixtle, vanilla, and amaranth and blend until smooth.
Add the ice and blend once more. Divide into two glasses.

* The *pixtle* is the pit inside the mamey fruit and it consists
of a hard outer shell enclosing an "almond." Crack open the
hard shell, remove the nut, and grate it the way you would
grate nutmeg.

⌂ ROSETTA,
LA PANADERÍA,
LARDO, CAFÉ NIN
(MEXICO CITY, MEXICO)
•
☺ LEA, 13; JULIETA, 11

snacks
mamey shake
↓

breakfast
black bean molletes
↳ p. 28

vegetable rice balls

Makes 14 rice balls

For the soybean sprout muchim:
3½ oz (100 g) soybean sprouts
Scant ½ teaspoon (1.5 ml) toasted
sesame oil
Scant ½ teaspoon (1 g) toasted
sesame seeds
Scant 1 teaspoon (1.5 g) minced scallion (spring onion), white part only
Pinch (0.5 g) of Himalayan pink salt

For the mu muchim:
3½ oz (100 g) mu (Korean radish)
or daikon radish
1½ teaspoons Himalayan pink salt
2½ teaspoons (10 g) sugar
Scant ½ teaspoon (1.5 ml) perilla oil
½ teaspoon (1.5 g) toasted
sesame seeds
Scant ½ teaspoon (1.5 g)
minced garlic
Scant 1 teaspoon (1.5 g) minced
scallion, white part only
Pinch (0.5 g) of Himalayan pink salt

For the spinach muchim:
3½ oz (100 g) spinach
1½ teaspoons Himalayan pink salt
½ teaspoon (2 g) minced garlic
1 teaspoon (2 g) minced scallion,
white part only
Scant ½ teaspoon (1.5 ml) toasted
sesame oil
Scant ½ teaspoon (1 g) toasted
sesame seeds

For the zucchini (courgette) muchim:
3½ oz (100 g) zucchini or
summer squash
1 teaspoon (5 ml) canola (rapeseed) oil
(or other neutral vegetable oil)
1½ teaspoons (5 ml) toasted
sesame oil
½ teaspoon (2 g) minced garlic
1 teaspoon (3 g) minced scallion,
white part only
½ teaspoon (3 g) Himalayan pink salt
Scant 1 teaspoon (2g) toasted
sesame seeds

Jumeok-bap are rice balls that are a favorite school lunch
or snack in Korea. When time or resources are tight, they
can be as simple as plain balls of rice. Or, as here, the rice can
be mixed with different vegetables, we call *muchim*, which
are then hidden by a coating of dried seaweed, giving them
the appearance of meteors.

•

Make the soybean sprout muchim:
Set up a bowl of ice and water. Bring a pot of salted water
to boil, blanch the soybean sprouts for 2 minutes, then
quickly drain and transfer to the cold water. When cooled
down, drain and gently squeeze to remove excess water.
Combine the sprouts with the remaining ingredients and toss
well to combine.

Make the mu muchim:
Finely julienne the mu. In a bowl, combine 1¼ cups (10 fl oz/
300 ml) water, sea salt, and sugar. Add the mu and soak
in this brine for 1 hour. Drain and gently squeeze to remove
excess water.

In a sauté pan, heat the perilla oil over medium heat. Add
the mu and the remaining ingredients and sauté until tender.
Season with salt and pepper to taste and let cool.

Make the spinach muchim:
Set up a bowl of ice and water. In a large pot of boiling water,
blanch the spinach for 1 minute. Then quickly drain and
transfer the spinach to ice water. When cooled down, drain
and gently squeeze to remove excess water. Combine the
spinach with the remaining ingredients and massage with one
hand to combine.

⌂ **BAROO (LOS ANGELES, CALIFORNIA, US)**
•
☺ **TAIHOON, 1**

<u>snacks</u>
vegetable rice balls
↓

<u>lunch</u>
full moon hotteok
↳ p. 52

For the soy seaweed sauce:
Generous ⅓ cup (3½ fl oz/100 ml) soy sauce
4 tablespoons shredded gim (also known as nori)
2 tablespoons rice vinegar
1 tablespoon toasted sesame oil
1 tablespoon toasted sesame seeds
2 teaspoons minced garlic
1 tablespoon minced scallions
1½ tablespoons Korean mirin

For the rice balls (or space rocks):
Toasted sesame seeds
Toasted sesame oil
Himalayan pink salt
6 cups (1 kg) cooked short-grain white rice (such as Koda Farms Kokuho Rose rice)
Shredded toasted gim (also known as nori)

Make the zucchini (courgette) muchim:
Chop the zucchini into cubes. Heat the canola (rapeseed) and sesame oils in a frying pan over medium heat. Add the garlic and scallion and allow to soften, approximately 1 minute. Add the zucchini and sauté until softened, approximately 3 minutes. Toss with the sea salt and sesame seeds and remove from the heat.

Make the soy seaweed sauce:
Blend all the ingredients.

Make the rice balls:
Chop each of the muchim into fine pieces. Toss the different muchim together and season with additional sesame seeds, sesame oil, and salt to taste. Then mix the vegetables into the rice in a ratio of 1 part vegetable to 3 parts rice. Use your hands to mix and make into balls of around 3 ounces (90 g) each. Cover a plate with the gim and roll each ball in the seaweed until the rice is completely covered.

Serve the soy seaweed sauce as a dipping sauce for the jumeok-bap.

duangporn "bo" songvisava and dylan jones

spring rolls

Makes 20 spring rolls

Makes 20 spring rolls

For the filling:
5 cilantro (coriander) roots, trimmed and cleaned
2 tablespoons chopped garlic
½ tablespoon ground white pepper
5 tablespoons rice bran oil
¼ cup (20 g) dried shrimp (prawns), rinsed in water
½ cup (20 g) dried shiitake mushrooms, soaked and then cut into thin strips
1 cup (70 g) julienned cabbage
1 cup (110 g) julienned carrot or daikon radish
3 tablespoons light soy sauce,* or to taste
3.5 g oz (100 g) ground (minced) pork
½ cup (60 g) cooked bamboo or jicama (optional)
½ cup (175 g) rice vermicelli noodles, soaked in water until soft
4 tablespoons light chicken stock
1 teaspoon raw sugar (optional)
2 tablespoons tapioca flour

For assembly:
1 tablespoon all-purpose flour
1 package (12 oz/340 g) spring roll skins
Neutral oil, for deep-frying

This snack, which both our kids love, is definitely Bo's inspiration. She loves origami and folding things and she loves that you can fit a ton of vegetables into the spring roll. Our kids, meanwhile, think they're fun to eat and, because they're fried, unhealthy. So it's a good trick.

●

Make the filling:

Pound the cilantro (coriander) roots, garlic, and white pepper together to make a coarse paste.

In a wok, heat the rice bran oil over high heat. Add the dried shrimp (prawns) and shiitake mushrooms. Fry until the shiitakes become golden brown. Add the cilantro/garlic paste and once the garlic is cooked, add the julienned cabbage and carrot with the soy sauce. Fry until the vegetables are cooked.

Add the pork and stir-fry constantly so the meat does not form lumps. Add the bamboo or jicama (if using) and fry for another 2 minutes. Add the soaked vermicelli to the wok along with 2 tablespoons of the stock. Stir well. Check the seasoning, adding the sugar and more soy sauce if desired.

In a small bowl, stir the remaining 2 tablespoons stock with the tapioca flour. Gently pour this mixture into the wok and cook to thicken the sauce.

Remove from the wok and refrigerate for 1 hour to chill.

To assemble:
When ready to assemble the rolls, make a light paste of water and flour to serve as a glue to seal the rolls. Place a spring roll skin on a work surface with a point facing you. Place about 3 tablespoons of the filling in the center of the wrapper. First fold the east-west corners to meet in the center. Then fold up

⌂ BO.LAN (BANGKOK,
THAILAND)
•
☺ DTAYCHIIT KEITH, 8;
DAYCHATHORN ETHAN, 5

snacks
spring rolls
↓

lunch
baked fish and rice
↳ p. 96

the south corner. Continue to fold the package over toward the north corner until a neat wrapper is formed. Use the water-flour paste to seal the edge. (Unfried rolls can be frozen in an airtight container for up to 3 months. They should be fried from frozen.)

Pour 3 inches (75 cm) neutral oil into a deep heavy pot and heat over medium-high heat to 350°F (180°C/Gas Mark 4).

Working in batches, fry until golden, 4–5 minutes. Serve hot.

* This is not lower-sodium soy sauce; the "light" is a reference to its lighter color. It is also called thin soy sauce.

elisabeth prueitt

quick bread-and-butter pickled vegetables

Makes 1 pint (16 fl oz/475 ml)

2 cups (280 g) assorted vegetables
(cucumbers, string beans, radishes,
onions, cauliflower)
½ cup (4 fl oz/120 ml) distilled
white vinegar
½ cup (4 fl oz/120 ml) apple cider
vinegar
½ cup (100 g) sugar
1½ teaspoons mustard seeds
(optional)
¾ teaspoon celery seeds (optional)
¼ teaspoon black peppercorns
¼ teaspoon crushed chili flakes
(optional)
¼ teaspoon ground turmeric
(optional)
6 whole cloves (optional)
1 cinnamon stick (optional)
1 tablespoon salt

❀ ◊ 🗄 ❀ ◎

"

If we're cooking together, I never tell
Archer if I think ingredients don't go
together—I let her mix and combine
as she likes so she can figure out
for herself what works. But if she's
strictly adhering to a recipe she finds
on social media, I ask her what would
happen if you left that out or added
this—to think as she goes.

"

This is a very quick and delicious recipe that is also very
flexible in the flavorings used; traditionally bread-and-
butter pickles have mustard and celery seeds and a pinch
of turmeric, but any combination can be used, including
the addition of chili flakes and cinnamon stick. All are
optional—add the spices you like, and make sure to use
a variety of vegetables. I like hot peppers, onions, carrots,
radishes, cucumbers. Beets (raw or lightly cooked) also
make a wonderful addition and will turn everything a beautiful
pink hue.

•

Place the vegetables in a 1-quart (32 fl oz /950 ml)
sterilized jar.

In a small saucepot, combine 1 cup (8 fl oz/250 ml) water,
both vinegars, the sugar, spices, and salt. Bring to a boil and
simmer for 5 minutes. Pour over the vegetables and cool.
Use immediately or store in the refrigerator.

HOUSE
OF
PICKLES

⌂ **TARTINE BAKERY (SAN FRANCISCO, LOS ANGELES, CALIFORNIA, US), TARTINE MANUFACTORY (SAN FRANCISCO, CALIFORNIA, US)**
•
☺ **ARCHER, 13**

<u>snacks</u>
quick bread-and-butter pickled vegetables
↓

<u>breakfast</u>
david eyres's pancake
↳ p. 34

max strohe
and ilona scholl

leek, cream, and stinking stones

Serves 4

Scant ⅓ cup (70 ml) buttermilk
2–3 egg yolks (1½ oz/46 g)
Scant ⅓ cup (70 ml) heavy (whipping) cream
3 large onions, halved and sliced
6 teaspoons canola (rapeseed) or other plant oil
1 teaspoon salt
1 leek
Oil, for the grill

For assembly:
1 black truffle (20 g) to shave
½ cup (4 fl oz/120 ml) Leek Oil (recipe follows) to taste

Makes 1½ liters (1.4 kg)

2¼ lb (1 kg) leek greens
6¼ cups (50 fl oz/1.5 liters) canola (rapeseed) oil

When Mimi was younger, she found truffles in our fridge and was disgusted with their smell. She asked, "What is wrong with us that we keep those stinky stones in the fridge?" So I [Max] decided to offer another perspective on them. When I was little, my favorite dish at my granny's house was creamed leek with potatoes. So I cooked that and threw in some truffles. Slicing the truffles thinly and placing them on something that was easy to fall in love with for a kid downright de-demonized the stinky stones and gave the truffles the opportunity to add some earthy and fragrant aroma to the leek. I told Mimi that we recreate a bit of the soil that the leek was growing in, to make it feel at home. She likes stinky stones now.

•

In a heatproof bowl set over a pan of simmering water, stir the buttermilk, egg yolks, and cream until the mixture breaks, starts to clump, and caramelizes slightly. Strain through a cheesecloth (muslin) and refrigerate overnight.

Put the onions in a large heavy-bottomed pan with the canola (rapeseed) oil and slowly caramelize until dark gold, 25–30 minutes.

Once caramelized, blend a scant ½ cup (100 g) of the onions at the highest speed until smooth, then taste and season with the salt. Pass through a sieve and let cool a bit, while covered. Place in a piping bag and keep warm.

Trim the dark green tops and root from the leek and remove the outer layers. Wash well and rub with some oil.

⌂ TULUS LOTREK
(BERLIN, GERMANY)
•
☺ EMILIA (MIMI), 10

snacks
leek, cream,
and stinking stones
↓

dinner
scallop, carrot,
and brown butter
↳ p. 184

Preheat a grill (barbecue) or grill pan. Set the leek on the grill over high heat. The outer layer should burn completely. As soon as the leek has burned evenly and bursts open, take it off the grill. Cut into even 1-inch (3 cm) pieces. Cover and cool down, then keep warm in a container.

To assemble:
Pipe 2 tablespoons of the cream mixture onto each plate. Then add 2 tablespoons of onion purée and 2 tablespoons of leek oil. Equally distribute the leeks between plates. Top each bowl with 1½ teaspoons (5 g) of shaved truffle.

•

Leek Oil

Cut the leek green into strips and wash. Mix with the oil and purée it little by little. Put the purée into a saucepan and heat over medium heat. The oil is finished when it has a deep green color, approximately 2 hours. Cool for 2 hours at room temperature and pass through a micro sieve.

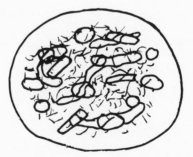

parsnip and apple soup

Serves 10–12

6 tablespoons margarine
3 cups (480 g) chopped sweet onions
2 leeks, cleaned and diced
2 fresh bay leaves
Salt
2½ lb (1.13 kg) parsnips, peeled and chopped
6 cups (48 fl oz/1.4 liters) chicken stock or vegetable stock
2 tablespoons apple cider vinegar
2 tablespoons local honey
4 Fuji apples; peeled, cored, and cut into ½ inch (1.25 cm) cubes
Freshly ground black pepper

In the fall, when parsnips get their first frost, they develop a nice sweetness. They're a staple in Newfoundland's culinary world and in my kitchen, too. My kids love parsnip and apple soup, sweetened with a little bit of honey. Hank and Iris love helping me prepare this in the kitchen. There are plenty of vegetables to peel and pots to stir. Because Hank has both a peanut and dairy allergy, this recipe forgoes the butter and cream, but the soup is rich enough without it. I like to make a big batch and freeze it, thawing and heating as we need.

•

In a Dutch oven (casserole dish), melt 4 tablespoons of the margarine over medium-heat. Add the onions, leeks, bay leaves and a pinch of salt and sweat for 5–7 minutes. Add the parsnips, stock, vinegar, 1 tablespoon salt, and 6 cups (48 fl oz/1.4 liters) water and bring to a boil. Reduce to a simmer, cover, and cook for 30 minutes.

Uncover, add the honey and apples, and continue to cook until tender, about 5 minutes. Season with salt and pepper, then stir in the remaining 2 tablespoons margarine. Purée with a hand blender. Garnish with reserved cubed apples.

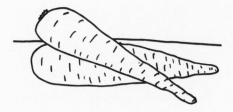

🏠 **RAYMONDS
(ST. JOHN'S,
NEWFOUNDLAND,
CANADA)**
•
☺ **HANK, 8; IRIS, 6**

<u>snacks</u>
parsnip and
apple soup
↓

<u>dinner</u>
moose boil-up
⤷ p. 192

lee anne wong

pork and chive dumplings

Makes 60 dumplings

For the dough:
4 cups (520 g) all-purpose (plain) flour
2 teaspoons salt
2 teaspoons toasted sesame oil

For the filling:
1½ lb (680 g) ground (minced) pork
1½ cups (75 g) garlic/Chinese chives,
sliced into ⅛-inch (3 mm) lengths
4 tablespoons ground pork fatback
¼ cup (2 fl oz/60 ml) reduced-sodium
soy sauce
¼ cup (2 fl oz/60 ml) Shaoxing rice
wine
2 tablespoons finely grated or minced
fresh ginger
2 teaspoons sugar
1 teaspoon salt
½ teaspoon ground white pepper

For the soy-ginger dipping sauce:
¼ cup (2 fl oz/60 ml) soy sauce
¼ cup (2 fl oz/60 ml) rice, black, or
Chinese red vinegar
1 tablespoon granulated sugar
2 tablespoons finely julienned
fresh ginger

For assembly:
Salt (depending on cooking method)
Flour (depending on cooking method)
Oil (depending on cooking method)
Chopped scallions (spring onions),
for garnish

This classic recipe is something I make in batches for my son, Rye. Homemade dumplings are obviously labor-intensive, but the good news is there's an economy of scale. I like to freeze the filling in small snack bags, pressed flat so they thaw quickly. One small snack bag should be enough filling for a dozen dumplings. Whenever he's hungry, I simply thaw the filling and either use dumpling wrappers or make my own dough. Rye loves playing with the dough, it's so tactile. How you cook these is up to you . . . they are delicious boiled, steamed, pan-fried, and deep-fried. (I've included directions for each.)

●

Make the dough:
In a saucepan, bring 2 cups (16 fl oz/475 ml) water to a boil. Meanwhile, sift together the flour and salt in a large bowl. Once the water is boiling, pour 1½ cups (12 fl oz/ 355 ml) of it into the flour, stirring well with a spoon. Add the sesame oil. Let sit for 3–4 minutes, then knead until smooth. (Add more water by the spoonful if the dough is not smooth.) Wrap in plastic wrap (cling film) and let sit for 1–2 hours.

Make the filling:
In a large bowl, combine the pork, garlic chives, fatback, soy sauce, Shaoxing, ginger, sugar, salt, and white pepper. Mix until well combined and homogeneous.

Make the dipping sauce:
Mix all the ingredients until the sugar dissolves. Refrigerate and allow to macerate for at least 1 hour.

Assemble and cook the dumplings:
Divide the dough into 60 balls and press into round wrappers ⅛-inch (3 mm) thick. Place 1 tablespoon pork filling in the center of each wrapper and pinch the edges closed.

<u>snacks</u>
pork and chive
dumplings
↓

<u>breakfast</u>
fruit kebabs
↳ p. 210

<u>Choose your cooking method:</u>
Boiled: Bring a large pot of salted water to boil over high heat. Add the dumplings in small batches, so as not to crowd the pot. Bring the water to boil and add ½ cup (4 fl oz/120 ml) cold water. Bring the water to boil again and add another ½ cup (4 fl oz/120 ml) cold water. When the water boils for the third time and the dumplings float, remove and serve.

Steamed: Steam on greased parchment paper over a boiling water bath, until the filling and dumpling skins are cooked through, about 4 minutes.

Pan-fried: In a liquid measuring cup, mix 2 cups (16 fl oz/475 ml) water and 2 tablespoons flour well until the flour has dissolved into the water and the mixture is cloudy. Heat a small nonstick pan over medium-high heat. Add 1 tablespoon of vegetable oil and place dumplings in the pan, lined up next to each other. Cook until the bottoms turn golden brown, 1–2 minutes. Add ½ cup (4 fl oz/ 120 ml) of the flour-water mixture to the pan; it will react with the hot pan and steam and splatter a bit—be ready with a tight-fitting lid. As soon as you add the flour-water mixture, cover the pan with the lid. Cook the dumplings, covered, until almost all the water has evaporated and a thin golden crust begins to form in the bottom of the pan. Uncover and cook until all water has evaporated. Carefully remove the dumplings, scrub the crust clean, and repeat.

Deep-fried: Pour 3 inches (7.5 cm) oil into a deep, heavy pot and heat to 350°F (180°C). Carefully drop the dumplings one by one into the hot oil, frying in small batches, being sure not to overcrowd the oil. Cook the dumplings until the filling is cooked and the exterior is golden brown, about 2 minutes. Drain on paper towels. Repeat with the remaining dumplings, making sure the oil temperature returns to 350°F (180°C) before frying again.

Serve the hot dumplings with the dipping sauce and garnished with scallions (spring onions).

lee anne wong

**james knappett
and sandia chang**

pork and zucchini dumplings

Makes 40 dumplings

17 oz (500 g) ground (minced) pork
1 large zucchini (courgette), shredded
on the large holes of a box grater
1 tablespoon grated fresh ginger
1 egg white
2 tablespoons oyster sauce
1 tablespoon soy sauce
Pinch of ground white pepper
40 Hong Kong–style dumpling
wrappers

A lot of times I [Sandia] feel like a single mother since James is so often at the restaurant. I'm constantly busy, which makes this a perfect option. Not only does it remind me of my own childhood, since my mum used to make these for me, but they're also easy to freeze ahead of time and cook when you can't be bothered cooking something à la minute. Depending how plump you make them, this will roughly make forty dumplings. For Shea I make them smaller, so it's easier for her to grab and is about two to three bites. I make them ahead of time and freeze them on a tray until frozen and transfer them to zip-seal freezer bags. This way there's always some ready in the freezer. Our daughter can polish off five or six of these at a time, but they're easy to make. My mother used to make her own dumpling wrappers, but I prefer just to purchase store-bought ones.

•

In a large bowl, combine the pork, zucchini (courgette), ginger, egg white, oyster sauce, soy sauce, and white pepper and mix together. My mother always recommends only mixing in one direction, making the meat filling less dense. Chill the mixture for 30 minutes before filling.

To fill each dumpling, place approximately 1 tablespoon of filling in the center of each wrapper. Fold the skin over and gather the edges, pressing to seal. (Moisten the edges with a bit of water or a mixture of cornstarch and water, if needed, to encourage sealing.)

Dumplings can be kept frozen in an airtight container for up to 3 months.

🏠 **BUBBLEDOGS,
KITCHEN TABLE
(LONDON, UK)**
•
☺ **SHEA, 1**

<u>snacks</u>
pork and zucchini
dumplings
↓

<u>dinner</u>
roast chicken
with noodles
↳ p. 170

Bring a large pot of water to a boil. Add the dumplings, working in batches, and boil for about 10 minutes.

Serve immediately. If desired, serve with dipping sauce.

pierre thiam

banana beignets

Serves 4

2 lb (910 g) peeled overripe bananas, peeled and mashed with a fork
1 lb (455 g) corn or fonio flour, sifted
2 tablespoons sugar
½ teaspoon active dry yeast
Pinch of salt
Pinch of ground cinnamon
Pinch of ground nutmeg
Grated zest of 1 lemon
1 tablespoon rum
2 cups peanut (groundnut) or other vegetable oil, for deep-frying

I love to serve this West African snack, called *talé talé*, to my kids. It's inspired by the banana beignets served in the streets of Benin City that my aunt used to prepare. Because they should be made with overripe bananas, it's the perfect way to use up those soft bananas with black spots that you haven't had a chance to eat.

•

In a large bowl, stir together the mashed banana, sifted flour, sugar, yeast, and salt. Stir in the cinnamon, nutmeg, lemon zest, rum, and 1 tablespoon of the oil.

Pour the rest of the oil into a large heavy pan and heat over medium-high heat until 450°F (230°C).

Working in batches, use a spoon or a small ice cream scoop to shape the batter into small balls and carefully drop into the hot oil. Fry evenly on all sides until golden brown and cooked through, 3–5 minutes. Remove with a slotted spoon and drain on paper towels.

Serve the beignets hot or at room temperature.

snacks

<u>snacks</u>
banana beignets
↓

<u>breakfast</u>
fonio coconut pudding
with fresh berries
↳ p. 42

manoella buffara

zucchini bread

Makes 1 loaf

1 cup (340 g) grated zucchini (courgette)
1 cup (120 g) whole wheat (wholemeal) flour
1 cup (120 g) chickpea (gram) flour
2 heaping tablespoons ground flaxseeds or chia seeds
¼ teaspoon grated nutmeg
1 pinch dried rosemary
3 tablespoons olive oil
1 teaspoon apple cider vinegar
1 tablespoon baking powder
¼ teaspoon salt
Savory granola or seeds, for sprinkling (optional)

❀ ◊ 🗍

"

My kids are always in the restaurant. It's so important they understand where the food come from, and why I'm cooking. I always tell the girls that I'm not going to work, I'm going change the world, because that is what I believe, and that's what I'm trying to teach them.

"

Whenever I make this bread, my kids wait outside the oven eagerly for it to emerge. It's not a matter of trying to hide the zucchini (courgette). In fact, whenever possible we use the zucchini that grows in our garden. When they first were exposed to zucchini, they were perhaps a little hesitant. But instead of praising them for trying, I encouraged them. Encouragement, I think, is much better than praise, for it is empowering. I encourage them to smell, taste, and touch the foods, to explore their own senses.

•

Preheat the oven to 400°F (200°C/Gas Mark 6). Grease an 8½ x 4½-inch (21.5 × 11.5 cm) loaf pan or line with parchment paper and grease the paper.

In a bowl, gently stir together the zucchini (courgette), both flours, ground flaxseeds, nutmeg, rosemary, ⅓ cup (2½ fl oz/80 ml) water, and the oil. Let it rest for about 10 minutes for the flaxseed to bind. In a small bowl, mix together the vinegar and the baking powder and add to the dough. Mix well.

Pour the batter into the pan. Sprinkle with granola or seeds if desired. Bake for about 30 minutes until a knife, inserted, is removed clean. Let cool for 5 minutes, then serve.

⌂ MANU (CURITIBA,
BRAZIL)
•
☺ HELENA, 5; MARIA, 3

snacks
zucchini bread
↓

treats
cocoa cookies
↳ p. 212

manoella buffara

didem şenol

zucchini fritters

Serves 2

4 zucchini (courgettes)
Salt
2 eggs
1¼ cups (200 g) all-purpose (plain) flour
1 teaspoon (4 g) baking powder
¾ cup (100 g) feta cheese
½ bunch fresh dill, chopped
½ bunch fresh parsley, chopped
Hazelnut oil for frying
Yogurt, for dipping

Mücver, or zucchini (courgette) fritters, are a very traditional Turkish dish. In the summertime, after swimming in the Black Sea, my kids love to come into the kitchen and steal a couple of these fritters. They think they're sneaky, but of course I know they're going to do it. And, since *mücver*—crispy on the outside, soft and creamy on the inside—are a great way to serve vegetables, I'm happy letting them think they're pulling a fast one on me.

•

Grate the zucchini (courgettes), add 1 hefty teaspoon of salt, and let sit in a colander to drain off excess liquid. Compress to remove as much liquid as possible

In a large bowl, combine the zucchini, eggs, flour, baking powder, and feta. Stir in the dill and parsley. Mix well, cover, and refrigerate the batter for 30 minutes.

When ready to fry, pour 3 inches (7 cm) oil into a large heavy-bottomed pan and heat to 375°F (190°C).

Place 1 tablespoon of batter into the oil and fry until golden, 5–6 minutes. Drain on paper towels. Serve hot with yogurt for dipping.

<u>snacks</u>
zucchini fritters
↓

<u>breakfast</u>
white cheese and
oregano dip on toast
↳ p. 48

margarita forés

rice porridge

Serves 4

4–6 tablespoons vegetable, sunflower, or corn oil
8–12 cloves garlic, finely chopped
1 medium white onion (about 3½ oz/100 g), thinly sliced
2½–3 oz (70–80 g) fresh ginger, peeled and thinly sliced
1 whole chicken (2¼–2 ¾ lb/1–1.2 kg) patted dry and cut into 10 pieces
1–2 tablespoon coarse sea salt
2½ cups (500 g) long-grain white rice, washed and drained
2 tablespoons fish sauce, preferably patis (Philippine fish sauce), plus more for serving
Black pepper, crushed in a mortar and pestle
Sea salt
2 oz (50 g) scallions (spring onions), finely chopped
8 calamansi halves or lime wedges

Arroz caldo, or literally "hot rice," is also known as *lugaw* in the Filipino language, or *pospas* in Ilonggo, the dialect spoken in my home province, Negros Occidental. It is a most comforting rice and chicken porridge that is a perfect *merienda* or midday snack in the Philippines. But most especially, it is a perfect dish to serve to children and even adults when they are not feeling well and in need of something simple and healthy to make them feel better.

In a small saucepan, warm half the oil over medium heat. Add half the chopped garlic and sauté until golden brown. Drain on paper towels and set aside for garnish.

In a large saucepan, warm the remaining oil over medium heat Add the remaining garlic, the onions, and ginger. Rub the chicken pieces with the salt, add to the pan, and brown slightly. Remove the chicken pieces from the pan (reserving all the cooking juices), set aside, and let cool. When cool, pull the meat off the bones, then shred the chicken. Transfer the chicken meat back to the saucepan with the sautéed garlic, onion, and ginger.

In a deep soup pot, combine the rice and 6¼ cups (50 fl oz/1.5 liters) water and bring to a boil. Stir constantly so the starch is released to thicken the soup. Once at a boil, reduce the heat to a simmer and cook for 30 minutes to reduce some of the liquid.

Add the garlic/onion/ginger/chicken mixture and all the juices saved from the previous saucepan to the rice and continue to simmer. Stir the fish sauce into the porridge. Adjust the seasoning with sea salt and crushed black pepper.

Serve the porridge in individual bowls, topped with the scallions, fried garlic bits, half a calamansi or a lime wedge, and some extra fish sauce on the side.

⭡ CIBO, LUSSO, GRACE
PARK (MANILA,
PHILIPPINES)
•
☺ AMADO, 29

<u>snacks</u>
rice porridge
↓

<u>dinner</u>
penne al telefono
↳ p. 146

elena arzak

spider crabs with sweet crackers

Serves 8

For the sweet crackers:
½ cup (100 g) dark brown sugar
2 cups (250 g) whole wheat flour
1 teaspoon (2.5 g) ground cinnamon
1 teaspoon (2.5 g) ground ginger
¾ teaspoon (1.5 g) ground cloves
Scant 1 teaspoon 2.5 g active dry yeast
Scant 2 teaspoons (12 g) honey
½ beaten egg white
Generous 2 teaspoons (12 ml) brandy
4 sticks plus 3 tablespoons (500 g) butter, melted
Salt

For the crab and its coral:
1 large spider crab
3 tablespoons olive oil
2 onions, finely chopped
1 tomato, peeled, seeded, and diced
½ cup (4 fl oz/120 ml) brandy
Salt

In San Sebastián, we are on the coast and we go to the beach whenever possible. Everyone searches for crabs as they scuttle into the sand. I remember doing it as a kid alongside my parents, just as my kids do it alongside me today. This dish, which I call Buscando Cangrejos—Searching for Crabs, is a play on that, something that my kids immediately understand and that connects them to our culture. We serve the spider crab on cookies at Arzak as an appetizer. I present it in a *salabardo*, or "hand net," with bits of seaweed clinging to the strands. But when I make it at home for my kids as a snack, I usually just place the cookies on the plate. (Who has a hand net lying around?) Anyway, they think the crab cookie is hilarious.

•

Make the sweet crackers:
In a bowl, stir together the sugar, flour, cinnamon, ginger, cloves, and yeast. Stir in the honey, 1 tablespoon plus 1 teaspoon water, the egg white, brandy, and melted butter. Add a pinch of salt and knead the dough well. Let stand 20 minutes.

Meanwhile preheat the oven to 350°F (180°C/Gas Mark 4). Line a baking sheet with parchment paper.

Once rested, roll out the dough to a thickness of ¼ inch (5 mm) and cut into approximately 24 crab-shaped cookies with the help of a crab-shaped cookie cutter or with a sharp knife and some effort. Bake for 10 minutes or until golden brown. Remove and let cool.

Prepare the crab:
Bring a large pot of water to a rolling boil. Boil the spider crab 7–10 minutes per pound (500 g).

snacks

⌂ ARZAK (SAN
SEBASTIÁN, SPAIN)
•
☺ NORA, 15; MATTEO, 14

snacks
spider crabs with
sweet crackers
↓

treats
chocolate-and-apple onion
↳ p. 208

Drain and when cool enough to handle, remove the spongy gray gills and stomach sac (located behind the jaws). Pick out the white flesh as well as the somewhat darker brown flesh. Clean the shell, and reserve.

In a large saucepan, heat the oil over medium heat until shimmering. Add the onions and sauté until translucent. Add the tomato and let everything stew for 20 minutes.

Add the spider crab meat and flambé with the brandy, and toss everything together. Let cook for 2 minutes over low heat. Add salt as needed.

To plate, mound the crab preparation on a few crab cookies.

frico with potatoes, cheese, and herbs

Serves 4

7 oz (200 g) potatoes
1 tablespoon olive oil
1 tablespoon minced pancetta
4¼ oz (120 g) grated T'minska cheese blend,* or hard full-fat cow's milk cheese
1 teaspoon minced herbs, such as oregano, tarragon, thyme, or lovage

🌾

I wake up in the morning working and I go to sleep working. I'm never home. So what I've tried to do is incorporate my family life into my work. It's not too difficult since we live right above the restaurant anyway. The restaurant kitchen is our family kitchen and the restaurant is our dining room. But no matter where we sit down, we use the time at the table as a moment to discuss what happened in school, in my children's athletic training, in their love lives. Whatever concerns they have personally, we talk about it, frequently over this easy-to-make, very comforting cheese-and-bacon hash called T'minska *frika*. It's very similar to frico, which hails from the other side of the Italian border in Friuli Venezia Giulia. I use a cow's milk cheese from Tolminc—hence T'minska in the name—a mix of year-aged and quite young cheeses, and I make this just before they get home from school.

•

Peel and grate the potatoes onto parchment paper. Steam in the oven for 8 minutes (100% steam) or in a regular oven at 350°F (180°C/Gas Mark 4) with a pan of water on the lower rack. Let the potatoes cool.

In a frying pan, heat the oil over medium-high heat. Add the pancetta and fry until crispy, about 2 minutes. Remove and set aside.

<u>snacks</u>
frico with potatoes, cheese
and herbs
↓

<u>dinner</u>
istrian stew
↳ p. 190

Add the potatoes and half the cheese to the pan and stir
well. When the cheese is melted, flip the entire thing like
an omelet. Add the remaining cheese, cover the pan,
and cook until both sides are golden brown, an additional
10–15 minutes. Serve hot garnished with the herbs.

* I use a blend of 80 percent 1-year aged cheese and
20 percent young cheese aged only 1–2 months.

roasted kelp with pajarito cream

rodolfo guzmán

Serves 6

7 oz (200 g) fresh kelp
⅔ cup (140 g) Pajarito Cream
(recipe follows)
½ cup (30 g) snipped chives
6 fresh basil leaves, finely chopped
¼ teaspoon freshly ground pepper

Kids don't normally eat seaweed, but one day I brought some *kollof* (a type of seaweed that grows only in Chile) home from the restaurant—where we had used it in a cream with *pajarito* (kefir), as an accompaniment to a baked witch potato atop a bed of oxalis blossoms. I didn't tell them it was seaweed, I simply roasted the kelp and served it alongside a mixture of kefir and cream. They loved it. It's quick, nutritious, and versatile. At home, we use *kollof* (*Durvillaea antarctica*), but any fresh kelp will do the trick.

•

Preheat the oven to 320°F (160°C/Gas Mark 3).

Spread the kelp on a sheet pan and bake for 15 minutes. Remove and let it cool at room temperature. Break into big pieces.

Whisk the pajarito cream vigorously and manually, until it looks shiny.

To plate, drop a quenelle of pajarito cream on the plate and add the chives, basil, and fresh pepper. To finish, hide a piece of kelp in the quenelle.

dinner
tortellini with chilean
mandarin béarnaise sauce
↳ p. 154

Makes about 3 cups (700 g)

Generous 2 cups (17 fl oz/500 ml)
heavy (whipping) cream
Generous ¾ cup (7 fl oz/200 ml) kefir

Pajarito Cream
Even though the pajarito cream makes more than you need
for the roasted kelp recipe, you need to make at least this
amount for the fermentation to be efficient. We use the
pajarito cream for absolutely everything, but it is especially
delicious on a bowl of fresh fruit at breakfast.

•

In a bowl, mix the cream and kefir. Transfer to a yogurt maker
and leave to ferment for 7 hours. Remove and let cool for
2 hours.

*

Gathering around the family dinner table is so self-evidently important that it has become shorthand for a healthy family life. Dinner table conversations. Dinner table politics. Dinner table bonding. And yet, fewer families are sitting around the table and those that do are doing so for shorter amounts of time. A recent study showed that when the fewer than one-third of American families *do* gather at mealtime, they meet for about twelve minutes, down from ninety minutes sixty years ago.

And yet for chefs, many of whom rely on the dinner rush to stay in business, dinner is the one meal for which they must absolutely be in the restaurant kitchen. Dinner is often where chefs shine. Dinner is the domain of creativity and brio. Richness and whimsy that might seem extravagant at lunch and obscene at breakfast is, at dinner, de rigueur.

For many chefs, Sunday dinner is the only dinner they have with their family and, as such, it is held reverently and taken seriously. It is not an afterthought. Rather it is the *telos* to which Sunday activity yields, whether those activities are visiting the farmers' market or harvesting vegetables from the patio garden.

Even without a busy restaurant kitchen, many of us non-chefs still have a hard time getting home or sitting down for dinner. Meetings and video chats that begin late, long commutes, or just plain grueling work hours keep us from the table. And when we do walk in the door, kids are often hungry and already losing it. Hours of prep time is a nonstarter and the very last thing you likely want to do. Though some of the recipes in this chapter are Sunday projects, most are, with some foresight, quick enough to have on the table before exhaustion, hunger, and a day's worth of stress combust into an all-family meltdown. And when dinner is served, the dinner table becomes a salve, a space of respite and of bonding. Many families, mine included, use the dinner table as a nightly clearinghouse. A well-laid one can be as restorative as a good night's sleep, into which we all tumble and deserve after the plates are cleared and the kids tucked in.

*

dinner

bonnie morales

raclette dinner with red wine-pickled onions

Serves 4

1 lb (455 g) German butterball potatoes (or other small creamy potato)
1–2 lb (455–910 g) raclette cheese
½ bunch broccoli rabe (rapini),*
cleaned and cut into 4-inch (10 cm)
sections
½ lb (225 g) high-quality cooked ham,
thinly sliced
½ lb (225 g) maitake mushrooms,
roasted
1 apple, cored and cut into ¼-inch
(6 mm) slices
4 oz (115 g) Red Wine–Pickled Onions
(recipe follows)
2–4 oz (55–115 g) cornichons
3 tablespoons whole-grain Dijon
mustard
1 baguette, sliced on a diagonal into
slices ⅓ inch (1 cm) thick
Squeeze bottle of neutral oil

Equipment
Tabletop raclette grill

Raclette fondue is one of those low-effort maximum-reward dinners. Kids love playing with their food. (Adults love playing with their food, too.) Not only is it an interactive dinner, but under the cover of melty cheese is a great way to sneak in more adventurous flavors—broccoli rabe! endive! leeks! Noah and Isaac also learn how heat affects various foods, so it's educational. Noah, for instance, lets the cheese go past the melty stage to form cheese chips (almost like frico). They both love putting cornichons in the pan with the cheese. There are no rules to a successful raclette dinner. Though it is true you'll need a special raclette machine—we use a Swissmar Stelvio eight-person raclette grill—you'll also be able to make an entertaining dinner for everyone in seconds that gives the kids an activity to do.

•

In a pot of boiling salted water, cook the potatoes until firm-tender. When cool, cut them in half.

Cut the cheese into slabs 2 × 3 inches (5 × 7.5 cm) and ⅛–¼ inch (3–6 mm) thick. Remove the rind if synthetic.

Arrange all the ingredients on platters or bowls. Turn on the raclette grill, per the manufacturer's instructions. Oil the cook top of the raclette grill as needed. Warm and/or cook items such as ham, vegetables, and potatoes on the cook top of the grill and place the cheese underneath in the grill's raclette dishes. When the cheese is melted, drape over the cooked vegetables, potatoes, and/or meat on your plate. Add pickled onions, mustard, or cornichons as desired. Play around with different combinations.

* Instead of broccoli rabe, this could be asparagus, green beans, Belgian endive (chicory), or leeks.

⌂ KACHKA (PORTLAND,
OREGON, US)
•
☺ NOAH, 10; ISAAC, 4

dinner
raclette dinner
with red wine-
pickled onions
↓

lunch
kasha varnishkes
↳ p. 84

Makes 3 cups

1 large sweet onion, halved, cored, and thinly sliced
2 cups (16 fl oz/475 ml) inky red wine, such as grenache
1 cup (8 fl oz/250 ml) distilled white vinegar
1 cup (8 fl oz/250 ml) apple cider vinegar
4 tablespoons salt
2 tablespoons sugar

"

We have a firm rule in our house that goes into effect from an early age: You have to try one bite of everything on your plate. This does not happen without tears but has been incredibly successful with both kids. One of the biggest mistakes that parents make is to stop offering a food because their child didn't like it once. Kids' taste buds are constantly changing and by preselecting what you think they like, you might be depriving them of an ingredient that they might now love.

"

Red Wine-Pickled Onions

Put the sliced onion in a large heatproof bowl and set aside.

In a saucepan, combine the wine, both vinegars, salt, and sugar and bring to a boil. Remove from the heat and immediately pour over the onions.

Let cool at room temperature and transfer to a storage container. Onions submerged in brine will keep for up to 1 month.

jocelyn guest
and
erika nakamura

beef and kale meatballs

Makes 40 meatballs

1 tablespoon flaxseeds*
1 tablespoon neutral oil
1 tablespoon unsalted butter
1 medium onion, chopped
1–2 cloves garlic, peeled
1 lb (455 g) coarse ground (minced) grass-fed beef
2 cups (100 g) kale (frozen is fine, you're tired)
¼ cup grated Parmesan cheese
¼ cup (60 g) sauce from grape tomato can
Chopped fresh basil
Salt and freshly ground black pepper

I [Jocelyn] tend to be the mom that freaks out about protein. When our daughter, Nina, was born, I emotionally prepared for eighteen years of trickery to get her to eat her vegetables, but, as we were anti-spoon feeding, I was scared that sautéed spinach or kale would drape its wily green body across Nina's throat, ending in certain doom. So I had to come up with an alternative way to get her those greens. Plus, Nina's allergic to eggs. Ergo this egg-free kale-rich recipe was born. What I like about this recipe is that you can make it in batches. In general, Erika is the à la minute chef and I'm the production sous. I'll make thirty carrot muffins or meatballs, freeze them, and just cook them when I need to.

•

In a small bowl, stir the flaxseeds with 3 tablespoons hot water and let stand until it absorbs the water and has plumped up.

In a frying pan, heat equal parts oil and butter over medium-low heat. Add the onion and slowly caramelize until dark, sweet and delicious, adding water to deglaze as necessary, about one hour. (You're a parent now, so caramelizing onion might not be on your to-do list. In that case, gently sauté until softened and translucent.) When cooked to your liking, Microplane the garlic into the pan. Cook until softened and incorporated, another 2–3 minutes. Pull from the heat, pop into a bowl, and then into the fridge to cool while you mix the meat.

⌂ J&E SMALL GOODS
(NORTH SALEM, NEW
YORK, US)
•
☺ NINA, 2

dinner
beef and kale meatballs
↓

breakfast
sourdough pancakes
↳ p. 30

In a large bowl, combine the beef, kale, Parmesan, tomato sauce, flax "egg," and basil. Season with salt and pepper. Mix everything together. Once cooled, add the cooked onion/garlic. Form the meatball mixture into about 1 tablespoon–size balls with a scoop or your hands.

At this point you can bake them for 15–20 minutes in a 325°F (160°C/Gas Mark 3) oven, or you can freeze raw for cooking later.

* I use the plumped-up flaxseed to substitute for the egg as a binding agent for the meatballs. If your kid is okay with eggs, just whisk an egg and add that. Ours isn't, so we use flax (which has added baby-genius benefits we've told ourselves).

suzanne goin
and david lentz

alex's bucatini and clams

Serves 4

1½ cups (85 g) fresh breadcrumbs
½ cup (4 fl oz/120 ml) plus 2 table-spoons extra-virgin olive oil
½ sprig rosemary
2 dried chiles de árbol or healthy pinch crushed chili flakes
2 cups (320 g) diced yellow onions
1 tablespoon fresh thyme leaves
Kosher (flaked) salt and freshly ground black pepper
¼ cup (40 g) sliced garlic
1 lb (455 g) bucatini, spaghetti, or linguine
3½ lb (1.6 kg) cockles or small Manila clams
¾ cup (6 fl oz/175 ml) dry white wine
4 tablespoons (60 g) unsalted butter
1 lemon, halved
½ cup (35 g) chopped fresh parsley

This is actually all the kids' favorite dish, but we've named it after our daughter, Alex. They ask for it often, which suits me [Suzanne] just fine, because, to be honest, bucatini with clams is one of my favorites, too. This was one of the first times I remember cooking something at home that both my husband, David, and I really wanted to eat and that the kids were excited about, too. I like to think of it as a crossover dish because it's pasta but, with the clams, it also has something more interesting going on. Plus the kids can really help in the kitchen with the clam shucking!

•

Preheat the oven to 375°F (190°C/Gas Mark 5).

Toss the breadcrumbs with 2 tablespoons of the olive oil, spread them on a baking sheet, and toast in the oven, stirring once or twice, until golden brown, 8–10 minutes.

Heat a large sauté pan over high heat for 2 minutes. Pour in the remaining ½ cup (4 fl oz/120 ml) olive oil, swirl the pan, and add the rosemary sprig and 2 chilies, crumbled with your hands. Let them sizzle in the oil about 1 minute or so, reduce the heat to medium, and add the onions and thyme. Season with 2 teaspoons salt and ¼ teaspoon black pepper. Cook for 3 minutes over medium heat, stirring often. Add the garlic and continue cooking until the onion and garlic are translucent and soft, another 3–4 minutes.

Meanwhile, bring a large pot of heavily salted water to a boil. Add the pasta to the rapidly boiling water and cook until al dente according to the package directions.

⌂ A.O.C., TAVERN,
LUCQUES CATERING
(LOS ANGELES,
CALIFORNIA, US)
•
☺ ALEXANDRA, 13;
JACK, 13; CHARLES, 11

dinner
alex's bucatini
and clams
↓

lunch
vegetable pistou
sandwiches
↳ p. 64

Add the clams to the onion mixture and toss to coat well. (If your pan is too small to accommodate all of the clams, divide them into two pans.) Add the wine, cover, and cook until the clams open, about 5 minutes or so. (After a couple minutes, lift the lid and gently stir the clams to help distribute the heat.) When all the clams have opened, remove the pan from the heat and use tongs or a slotted spoon to remove them to a bowl. Discard any unopened clams. When they're cool enough to handle, take half the clams out of their shells and put in a bowl. (If you like, you can skip this step and serve all the clams in their shells.)

Reserving 1 cup (8 fl oz/250 ml) of the cooking water, drain the pasta and add to the pan, tossing the noodles well. Return the pan to medium-high heat for 3–4 minutes to reduce the juices and coat the noodles. If the noodles seem dry, add a little of the reserved pasta water, letting it cook down 1–2 minutes to thicken the sauce. Add the butter, a big squeeze of lemon juice, shucked clams, parsley, and ¼ teaspoon salt. Toss well and taste for seasoning.

Arrange the pasta on a large warm shallow platter and scatter the clams still in their shells over the noodles. Sprinkle the breadcrumbs over the pasta.

ben shewry

summer tomato sauce

Makes 1 quart (1 liter)

Scant ½ cup (3½ fl oz/100 ml) olive oil
3½ oz (100 g) garlic, peeled and thinly sliced
5½ lb (2.5 kg) very ripe tomatoes, cut into chunks
Salt
Superfine (caster) sugar (optional)
Freshly ground black pepper

"

I try to be patient with my kids and don't force them to eat things they don't want to. But my kids have great diversity in their diets and my partner, Kylie, and I change up their meals all the time. It's rare to eat the same thing twice—this naturally leads to them being open-minded eaters. We always try to give the kids the cultural context for the food that we eat at home, too. All food is filled with stories of humans from all over the world. It's really fascinating and it's important that they understand where recipes and ideas come from.

"

This sauce is a staple at home. It's brilliant ladled generously over buttered pasta, as a sauce for grilled lamb meatballs, with baked eggs, or as a sauce for pizza. It's easy to make and infinitely better for you than the store-bought variety and it tastes better, too. My partner, Kylie, and I always try and make too much—which is hard because it always gets eaten— and keep a container in the freezer for time-poor nights. It's best made during the summer, when tomatoes are plentiful and affordable. It can be kept for up to three months frozen.

•

In a large saucepan, heat the oil over low heat. Add the garlic and gently cook until tender, approximately 5 minutes.

In a blender, purée the tomatoes until smooth. Add the tomato purée to the garlic and season with salt to taste. Simmer for 20–30 minutes to reduce by about half.

Taste and if the sauce is too acidic—this depends on how ripe your tomatoes are—add a small pinch of sugar to balance the acid. Season to taste with salt and black pepper to finish.

<u>dinner</u>
lamb curry
↳ p. 178

ben shewry

pasta with tomato and anchovy sauce

alex atala

Serves 4

½ white onion
2 teaspoons capers
5 anchovy fillets
⅓ cup (2¾ fl oz/80 ml) olive oil
1½ cups (12 fl oz/350 ml) strained
tomatoes (passata)
14 oz (400 g) pasta

This recipe has been with me for thirty years now. I picked it up when I was working at Sancho Panza, an osteria in Milan, and it still brings back memories of my time in Italy. Before I had kids, it was a dish I used to cook for family meal for my team in many restaurants. So naturally, I continued to cook it for my children, family, and friends. It's always a hit.

•

In a blender, combine the onion, capers, anchovies, and olive oil and process until the texture looks like a cream. Set aside.

In a large saucepan, heat the tomato sauce over low heat until it reduces by half.

Meanwhile, in a large pot of boiling salted water, cook the pasta according to package directions.

When the pasta is almost ready, add the anchovy cream to the tomato sauce. Drain the pasta, add to the sauce, and be happy.

⌂ **D.O.M.**
(SÃO PAULO, BRAZIL)
•
☺ **PEDRO, 25; TOMÁS,**
18; JOANA, 18

<u>dinner</u>
pasta with tomato
and anchovy sauce
↓

<u>treats</u>
dona palmyra cake
↳ p. 198

margarita forés

penne al telefono

Serves 6–8

Salt
17 oz (500 g) penne pasta
2 cups (16 fl oz/475 ml) tomato sauce,
homemade or store-bought
2 cups (16 fl oz/475 ml) heavy cream
4 tablespoons (60 g) butter
Sea salt and freshly ground black
pepper
3½ oz (100 g) mozzarella cheese, cut
into ½-inch (1.25 cm) cubes
¾ cup (50 g) crumbled Filipino white
cheese or ricotta
3½ oz (100 g) Parmigiano-Reggiano
cheese, freshly grated
1 bunch fresh sweet basil leaves
(reserve a sprig for garnish)
Freshly grated nutmeg
Chili flakes

This pasta dish is something my son, Amado, and other children loved growing up. It is a tomato-based pasta but with cream, and is made more hearty with melted mozzarella, Filipino white cheese, and Parmigiano-Reggiano. Some torn basil leaves add a refreshing touch to the dish. For younger children, a smaller pasta shape like ditalini could be a good alternative.

In a pot of salted boiling water, cook the pasta to al dente according to package directions.

Meanwhile, in a deep heavy saucepan, warm the tomato sauce over medium heat. Stir in the cream and butter and cook until the sauce thickens. Season with sea salt and pepper to taste.

Reserving a little of the pasta cooking water, drain the pasta and transfer to the tomato-cream mixture with some of the pasta water. Add the mozzarella and white cheese and let melt. Add half the grated Parmigiano. Toss and blend well.

Tear the fresh basil leaves and add to the pasta. Season with nutmeg and chili flakes to taste. Adjust the seasoning with sea salt and black pepper.

Transfer to a warm serving platter. Top with the remaining grated Parmigiano-Reggiano, garnish with a basil sprig, and finish with freshly ground black pepper. Serve immediately.

PENNE FOR YOUR THOUGHTS.

dinner

dinner
penne al telefono
↓

snacks
rice porridge
↳ p. 126

beverly kim
and johnny clark

lentil bolognese with spaghetti squash

Serves 4

1 cup black caviar lentils
One 10-inch (25 cm) long whole spaghetti squash
2 medium carrots, sliced
1 medium Vidalia (sweet) onion, sliced
1 stalk celery, sliced crosswise
3 cloves garlic, peeled
¼ cup (2 fl oz/60 ml) good olive oil
1 quart (280 g) fresh shiitake mushrooms, sliced
2 tablespoons chopped fresh oregano
1 cup (8 fl oz/250 ml) red wine, such as Barolo
2 cups (16 fl oz/475 ml) vegetable stock or beef stock
1 can (28 oz/795 g) San Marzano tomatoes, pulsed into a rough pulp in a food processor
4 tablespoons tomato paste (purée)
½ cup whole-milk ricotta cheese (preferably buffalo ricotta from Italy)
¼ cup (2 fl oz/60 ml) heavy (whipping) cream
Salt and freshly ground black pepper
Lots of fresh basil leaves, for garnish
Grated Parmigiano-Reggiano cheese, for garnish

Daewon, our eldest, is the most likely to try vegetables. Hanul lives on mac-and-cheese and the baby is the baby. But everyone, including us, loves Bolognese. At home, we find nearly infinite variations of the dish, depending on what we have on hand. Often we'll use ground beef or pork, but in this preparation we happened to have lentils in the pantry and spaghetti squash in the fridge. The latter is another way of getting vegetables into our kids' bodies, not sneakily but perhaps cleverly. The important thing here is not to overcook the squash or else it will become mushy. We've found our kids are very sensitive—like many are—to texture. Watery squash is a major turnoff, but when cooked just enough that the strands are still intact, it's a major hit.

•

Soak the lentils in in 1 quart (32 fl oz/950 ml) of water overnight. Cook them in the soaking water until just soft, 15–20 minutes. Drain and set aside.

Cut the squash crosswise into 2-inch (5 cm) wide rings and remove the seeds. Put one ring at a time on a microwave-safe plate and pour 3–4 tablespoons water over the squash. Microwave on high for 2 minutes, or until the strands of the squash are just starting to separate. To test, use a fork to see the strands start to separate without breaking. It should still be slightly challenging to separate the strands. You want to keep them a little crunchy so they don't get soggy. Set the ring aside intact (you'll separate the strands later). Repeat this process until all the rings have been cooked.

In a food processor, combine the carrots, onion, celery, and garlic and pulse until a couscous-like consistency.

Preheat a fairly large heavy pot, like an enamel Dutch oven (casserole), over medium-high heat. Add the olive oil, mushrooms, and carrot/onion/celery/garlic mixture. Cook this down for 25–30 minutes, stirring constantly so it doesn't burn. You're looking for some good caramelization.

Add the oregano and continue to cook for another 5 minutes. Add the red wine and stock and cook for 10–15 minutes.

Reduce the heat to medium and add the blitzed canned tomatoes and the tomato paste (purée), and cook for 15–20 minutes.

Add the lentils and cook until the lentils start to fall apart slightly. Don't overdo it. The sauce should be fairly thick, like chili. Finally, add the ricotta and cream, reduce the heat to low and simmer gently. Season with salt and pepper to taste.

Take a fork and scrape all the spaghetti squash strands from the skin. Put all the strands onto a plate and spread evenly. Drain off any excess water and microwave until hot, about 1 minute.

To serve, divide the squash and spoon the sauce over. Garnish with lots of fresh basil and Parmigiano.

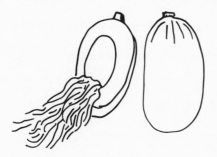

will goldfarb

pasta with chickpeas

Serves 2

For the sauce:
¼ cup (2 fl oz/60 ml) olive oil
1 red onion, finely diced
Salt
Scant 1 cup (200 g) canned chickpeas (half a 15 oz/425 g can), liquid reserved
2 cloves garlic, smashed with the palm of your hand and peeled
Dash of pimentón or smoked sweet chili powder
Drop of sherry vinegar
Thin slice stale bread, finely diced
Scant 1 cup (200 g) canned whole tomatoes (half a 14 oz/400 g can)
Parmesan rind (optional; if handy)
Splash of milk (optional)

Optional add-ins:
3½ oz (100 g) button mushrooms, diced
Salt
Olive oil
Vinegar
1 oz (25 g) bitter greens, thinly sliced

For finishing:
5–6 oz (150–180 g) rigatoni pasta
Olive oil
Salt
Parmesan cheese, for grating

Whenever we are hungry, which is basically always, I whip up a bowl or pot of this satisfying pasta. I was first turned onto this dish by my wife, who grew up in Rome. Although at first I didn't understand how you could have chickpeas and pasta together, eventually my daughter and I grew to love it, and now literally crave it. We can survive on this alone. You could pick up a better version in Rome at Armando al Pantheon, Augusto, or even better, Santo Palato by Sarah Cicolini, but this one suits us fine.

•

Make the sauce:
In a large saucepan, heat the olive oil over medium heat. Add the onion, lightly salt, and cook down until translucent, approximately 5 minutes.

Meanwhile, in a small pan, heat the reserved chickpea liquid with the garlic cloves. At the same time, feel free to get a medium pot of heavily salted water to a rolling boil for the pasta.

When your onion is all the way broken down, but still golden (like me), season lightly with pimentón and a drop of vinegar.

Fry the bread in the caramelized onion-and-oil base until golden (still like me). Add the chickpeas, moisten with a bit of plain or salted water, and bring to a good boil. Add the tomatoes and get it really going. (Feel free to add Parmesan rind if using.) If you find the acidity too strong, a splash of milk is always nice.

Add the chickpea/garlic water and return to a boil. Simmer until the sauce just comes together, about 15 minutes.

<u>dinner</u>
pasta with chickpeas
↓

<u>breakfast</u>
vegetable frittata
↳ p. 26

<u>If desired, make the optional garnishes:</u>
In a dry frying pan, cook the mushrooms down with salt, then splash with a little olive oil and a drop of vinegar. Steam the bitter greens. Set both aside.

<u>To finish:</u>
Cook the pasta in the boiling salted water until al dente according to the package directions. Reserve a bit of the pasta cooking water, drain the pasta and return it to the same pan. Season with olive oil and salt, then dress with the mushroom and bitter greens if using.

Hit the pasta with as much sauce as it can absorb. Bump it up with some of the reserved pasta cooking water if necessary.

Bowl it up and top with as much grated cheese as you have. Enjoy.

will goldfarb

smoked sweet potato gnocchi

jonny rhodes

Serves 4

2 tablespoons olive oil
1 lb (455 g) sweet potatoes
Salt
4 tablespoons (60 g) unsalted butter, melted
1¼ cups (115 g) grated Parmesan cheese
1¼ cups (330 g) sifted whole wheat (wholemeal) flour

Equipment
Smoker

My kids love sweet potatoes and yams, but they often associate them with candied yams, a soul food staple. With this dish, I want them to experience sweet potatoes in a different way, without all that sweetness. What better way than in gnocchi, in this recipe I developed while in culinary school. It's still one of my favorites.

•

Lightly oil the sweet potatoes and season with salt.

Set up a smoker and let it come to 225°F (107°C). Add the sweet potatoes, cover, and smoke for 1 hour 10 minutes. (This can also be done on a grill.) When cool enough to handle, peel and reserve the skin.

In a food processor, purée the smoked sweet potatoes, melted butter, and salt to taste.

In a bowl, combine the Parmesan, sweet potato purée (½ cup at a time), flour, and more salt to taste. Knead the dough as you go to work in any dry patches, but do not over knead into a tough dough.

After your dough is formed and ready, place it into 9½ x 5-inch (24 x 13 cm) bread loafs pans and allow to rest, covered, for 1 hour in the refrigerator.

Remove the dough and cut into 3-inch-thick (7.5 cm) slices. Stretch and roll each slice into a thick rope 12–18 inches (30–45 cm) long. Cut the rope crosswise into 1-inch (2.5 cm) gnocchi nuggets.

AS FLUFFY AS CLOUDS

dinner

<u>dinner</u>
smoked sweet
potato gnocchi
↓

<u>lunch</u>
chili mac and cheese
↳ p. 82

Set up a bowl of ice and water. Bring a pot of seasoned water
to a boil. Working in batches, blanch the gnocchi until they
begin to float, then scoop the floating gnocchi out of the water
with a skimmer and plunge into the ice bath for 15 seconds.
Place all the blanched gnocchi to drain on paper towels.

Either serve immediately or cover and refrigerate for up to
2 days. (Gnocchi can also be frozen for up to 6 weeks.)

tortellini with chilean mandarin béarnaise sauce

Serves 6

For the Béarnaise sauce:
2 eggs
⅛ teaspoon (1 g) sea salt
⅛ teaspoon (1 g) freshly ground black pepper
2 Chilean mandarins or limes
3½ tablespoons (50 g) unsalted butter
1 shallot, diced
½ teaspoon (0.5 g) dried oregano
1 tablespoon plus 2 teaspoons rice vinegar

For the pasta:
2¼ lb (1 kg) cheese tortellini
Olive oil, for drizzling
⅓ cup (30 g) snipped chives
2½ oz (70 g) Parmesan cheese, shaved

This is not something that I make by choice. After one of our Sunday dinners, my little ones simply decided this would be their favorite recipe and so it has been. I've always found Béarnaise a bit heavy, so in this recipe I've adapted it by using the entire egg—not just the yolk, as is customary—adding a bunch of vinegar and incorporating a touch of citrus. In autumn, we use the zest of Chilean mandarin, a citrus that is very similar to yuzu. But the zest of any green citrus does well, too. One of the reasons my kids—and I—have grown to love this is that the sauce is very accommodating to whatever type of citrus you might have at home. The method of making the bearnaise is very much informed by the idea that I don't want to—and can't—spend too much time prepping. So I use the boiling pasta water as the bain marie to make the sauce. By the time the pasta is ready so is the sauce, bursting with flavor.

•

Make the Béarnaise sauce:
In a stand mixer, beat the eggs at high speed until frothy. Add the salt and pepper. Grate in the zest of the Chilean mandarin.

In a small pan, melt the butter completely, stirring slowly over low heat, then whisk into the eggs until emulsified. In the same pan used to melt the butter, add the shallot, oregano, and rice vinegar. Let reduce over low heat for 2 minutes. Strain the liquids quickly into the egg mixture, pressing with a spoon over the shallots to extract the flavor, but reserving the shallots themselves.

Make the pasta:
Meanwhile, bring a pot of water to a boil. As the water is boiling, place the bowl with the Béarnaise atop it and whisk until the Béarnaise thickens and becomes silky. Once ready, add the tortellini to the boiling water and cook until al dente.

CHILEAN
MANDARIN

<u>dinner</u>
tortellini with chilean
mandarin béarnaise sauce
↓

<u>snacks</u>
roasted kelp
with pajarito cream
↳ p. 132

To serve, arrange the tortellini in the center of the plates.
Drizzle olive oil over the pasta, add 2 large tablespoons of
Béarnaise sauce, and sprinkle with the chives and shaved
Parmesan. Serve immediately.

potato dauphinois

Serves 6

1 cup (8 fl oz/250 ml) milk
3 cups (24 fl oz/750 ml) heavy (whipping) cream
1½ cloves garlic, crushed, plus ½ clove
3½ tablespooons (50 g) unsalted butter, cold and cubed, plus butter for greasing
1 cup (30 g) lovage
Sarawak pepper
2 lbs (1 kg) starchy potato, peeled and cut into 1/10-inch (3 mm) thick slices

"

My son dares to explore new taste territories through the garden. For example, by starting our own tomato seedlings, and with a vegetable garden very much oriented toward aromatic plants, he discovers and I am inspired at the same time. Through playfulness, a spirit of discovery and understanding, he grasps the raw product, which comes from nature. He is in tune with the times, because with two friends he creates recipes, makes them live, edits them, and publishes them online. He is interested in many products from all over the world. He is passionate about all fields, especially pastry, and he challenges himself with recipes. Nathan now realizes that the more you do, the more you master.

"

This is a recipe that comes from the Drôme region, in southeastern France, where my family is from. It has been passed down from my great-grandmother to my grandfather to my parents to me and now to my son. It's a delicious and, more important, easy-to-make dinner. I don't want my home to become my second workplace—the cooking is fun, spontaneous, and relaxed.

•

Preheat the oven to 350°F (180°C/Gas Mark 4).

In a large heavy-bottomed saucepan, combine the milk and cream with the crushed garlic, lovage, and a little Sarawak pepper. Bring to a boil and season with a pinch of salt.

Meanwhile, rub a casserole dish with the half clove of garlic, then grease with butter and set aside.

Once the milk-and-cream mixture is simmering, add slices of potato and allow to cook for 8 minutes over low heat. Then remove and place in the buttered casserole dish. Continue to reduce the milk and cream for another 5 minutes. Then pour that into the dish atop the potatoes as well.

If you have time, let the mixture rest for 1 hour. If you're in a hurry, top with the small cubes of cold butter and bake in the oven for 15 minutes. Remove, let cool slightly, then serve.

dinner

⌂ **MAISON PIC**
(VALENCE, FRANCE)
•
☺ **NATHAN, 13**

<u>dinner</u>
potato dauphinois
↓

<u>treats</u>
floating islands
with rose praline
↳ p. 204

danny bowien

rice cake soup with brisket jus and seaweed

Serves 4

For the soup:
1 piece (5 inches/12 cm) of dashi kombu
2 cups (16 fl oz/475 ml) clam juice
4 tablespoons instant dashi powder
1 teaspoon salt
Freshly ground black pepper
4 cups sliced Korean rice cakes

For finishing:
1 lb shredded Overnight Brisket (recipe follows) or mushrooms of your choice, thinly sliced
2 packages (2.2 oz/62 g each) salted Korean seaweed snacks (sesame-flavored)
4 cups Chinese broccoli or bok choy, blanched
4 tablespoons slivered scallions (spring onions)

This is Mino's favorite soup and a dish I know he will always eat. It's really easy for me to make for his dinner because I usually grab brisket and rice cakes from the restaurant on my way home. It's simple, hearty, and filling. The recipe for the brisket is the same we use for Mission's classic Broccoli Beef Brisket. It's fairly labor-intensive (which is why I bring it home from work), so if you want to forego the overnight cook and take the path of least resistance, use mushrooms, alongside a good seafood or clam broth. Both options are included.

•

Make the soup:

In a large pot, combine the kombu, clam juice, dashi powder, salt, and 1½ gallons (5½ liters) water and bring to a boil. Taste for seasoning and adjust to taste with more salt and some pepper. Add the rice cakes and remove from the heat.

Portion the brisket or mushrooms into four bowls. Equally divide the soup across the bowls. Garnish with the seaweed snacks, Chinese broccoli, and scallions (spring onions).

YOU LOOK SHREDDED.

WE'VE BEEN UP ALL NIGHT.

🏠 MISSION CHINESE
FOOD (NEW YORK,
NEW YORK, US)
•
☺ MINO, 6

dinner
<u>dinner</u>
rice cake soup
with brisket jus
and seaweed
↓

<u>treats</u>
sweet potatoes with
milk, peanuts, and
maraschino cherries
↳ p. 216

<u>Serves 4</u>

½ cup (4 fl oz/120 ml) Dijon mustard
1 tablespoon soy sauce
2½ lb (1.13 kg) beef brisket,
untrimmed
2 tablespoons salt
2 teaspoons freshly ground black
pepper

<u>Overnight Brisket</u>
In a bowl, whisk together the mustard and soy sauce. Rub the brisket with the mustard-soy compound until completely coated. Sprinkle with the salt and pepper. Allow the brisket to cure, refrigerated, for a minimum of 2 hours and up to 12 hours.

Bring a grill (barbecue) to high heat. Let the brisket come to room temperature.

Place the brisket on the grill and char over high heat until blackened, but not cooked through, about 5 minutes per side. (It should resemble a nicely blackened steak.) Remove from the heat and allow to cool for 10 minutes. Then wrap in plastic wrap (cling film) followed by foil. Transfer the wrapped brisket to a shallow baking dish and place in the oven on the lowest setting—about 180°F (82°C)—for 12 hours or overnight.

Once cooked, the brisket should be very tender. Reserve liquids for the soup.

lemongrass clams

Serves 4

5 lemongrass stalks
2 teaspoons vegetable oil
5 slices fresh ginger
1 tablespoon minced garlic
4½ lb (2 kg) clams, cleaned*
Chicken bouillon powder
Fish sauce
½ oz (10 g) Vietnamese basil
(húng quế)

Da Nang is a beach city, so we eat a lot of seafood, especially shellfish. This dish, with the addition of chili, which we omit for Arya, is very traditional. These clams are both fun and easy to make. Arya loves to stand next to me tossing the herbs into the pot. She also loves watching the clams pop open. I explain to her that this aromatic soup can also help cure a cold or flu.

•

Bruise the lemongrass with a knife or pestle and cut into 1¼-inch (3 cm) pieces.

Heat a medium pot over medium heat. Add the oil, ginger, lemongrass, and garlic and fry until aromatic but not browning. Add the clams and 3 cups (24 fl oz/750 ml) water to the pot. Season with chicken powder and fish sauce to taste. Cover and steam until the clams have opened. Add the basil and serve hot.

* Soak the clams in salt water for 30 minutes with a bit of chili to release impurities.

🏠 **NÉN RESTAURANT (DA NANG, VIETNAM)**
•
☺ **ARYA, 5**

<u>dinner</u>
lemongrass clams
↓

<u>lunch</u>
morning glory stir-fried
with garlic
↳ p. 74

butter shrimp and taro wedges

Serves 4

For the amadumbe wedges:
9 oz (250 g) amadumbe (taro root)
Salt
2 teaspoons olive oil

For the shrimp (prawns):
2 teaspoons (3 g) finely chopped fresh parsley
1 tablespoon (3 g) finely chopped chives
1 tablespoon (3 g) finely chopped fresh cilantro (coriander)
Salt and red peppercorns
2½ tablespoons (40 g) salted butter
2 teaspoons olive oil
6 extra-jumbo shrimp (king prawns), deveined
1 large clove garlic, finely minced

For the salad:
3½ oz (100 g) radishes, thinly sliced
1 small carrot, finely diced
1 small red onion, finely diced
¼ small yellow bell pepper, finely diced
¼ small red bell pepper, finely diced
3 oz (80 g) lettuce
3½ tablespoons freshly squeezed orange juice
2 teaspoons (5 g) baobab powder
¾ cup (6 fl oz/175 ml) olive oil
Salt and freshly ground black pepper

For the garnish:
Fresh dill
Edible flowers

Bhongo loves his indigenous dishes. For example, he can smell his dumplings, *imfino*, and oxtail from a mile away as he approaches the house. Being born on the east coast of the country, and having been exposed to seafood from a young age, it makes sense that he absolutely adores shrimp (prawns)—and to my surprise, oysters, too. *Amadumbe*, or taro, which is rich in calcium, is a tastier option for us than the potato. This dish is generally our Friday dinner option: quick to prepare, light, healthy, and mouthwatering.

•

Cook the amadumbe:
Preheat the oven to 400°F (200°C/Gas Mark 6).

In a saucepan, combine the amadumbe and just enough salted water to cover. Bring to a boil and cook until tender, 5–8 minutes. (Taro roots cook like potatoes, however depending on their size, they generally cook more quickly.) Drain them and cut into wedges.

Place them on a baking sheet and lightly brush them with the olive oil. Transfer to the oven and bake until golden, about 15 minutes.

Prepare the shrimp (prawns):
Finely chop and combine the parsley, chives, cilantro (coriander), salt, and red peppercorns. In a frying pan, heat the butter and olive oil over medium heat. Add the shrimp (prawns) and garlic and cook until the prawns are golden, about 5-8 minutes. Flip the shrimp over and fry for about 2 minutes and immediately remove from the heat. Sprinkle with the herb and peppercorn mixture.

dinner
<u>butter shrimp</u>
and taro wedges
↓

lunch
<u>lemony chicken</u>
with insima
↳ p. 92

Make the salad:
In a large bowl, toss together the radishes, carrot, red onion, both bell peppers, and lettuce. In a small screw-top jar, combine the orange juice, baobab powder, olive oil, a pinch of salt, and black pepper to taste. Close and shake the jar vigorously until well mixed.

Add the dressing to the salad just before serving.

Serve the prawns alongside a few wedges of amadumbe and a side salad, garnished with dill and edible flowers.

yoshihiro narisawa

miso-marinated cod

For the cod:
2 cod fillets (2½ oz/70 g each)
Salt
½ cup (4 fl oz/120 g) sake
2 teaspoons (10 ml) soy sauce
4 tablespoons salt-packed capers, rinsed
1 tablespoon olive oil
3 tablespoons plus 1 teaspoon heavy (whipping) cream
Generous ¾ cup (7 fl oz/200 ml) milk
½ cup (35 g) minced herbs, such as shiso, dill, and parsley

For the salted ponzu sauce:
3 cups (25 fl oz/750 ml) sake
¾ cup (6 fl oz/175 ml) mirin
3 teaspoons salt
juice of 1 citrus
2½ tablespoons (40 g) raw (brown) sugar
4¾ teaspoon (2 fl oz/65 ml) sesame oil
¼ teaspoon roasted sesame seeds

By marinating the fish in miso, the excess water of the raw fish is extracted by the salt, and at the same time the umami of the miso is transferred into the fish. Often this dish is left to marinate for hours, but at home I find this quick marinade still works. The capers—both whole and in a cream sauce—add a richness and depth of flavor that my kids and I love.

•

Cook the cod:
Rinse and pat the cod fillets dry. Generously sprinkle with salt and wrap in cheesecloth (muslin). Slather the miso over the cloth and refrigerate for 20 minutes so the miso permeates the fish.

Meanwhile, using a mortar and pestle or in a mini food processor, purée 2 tablespoons of the capers (set the remainder aside whole).

Unwrap the fish. In a nonstick frying pan, heat the oil over medium heat. Add the fish and cook until opaque, 7–9 minutes, turning once.

Meanwhile, in a small saucepan, combine the cream, caper purée, and a pinch of salt and heat over medium heat until until boiling.

In a separate pan, bring the milk to a boil over medium heat, stirring frequently, until the milk reaches 140°F (60°C). Remove from the heat and let cool for 1 minute. Skim the skin from the milk and add to the sauce, stirring to incorporate.

Make the sauce:
Combine the sake and mirin in a small pot. Bring to a boil and let reduce for 5 minutes. Add the salt, citrus, sugar and sesame oil, stirring until dissolved. Let cool slightly. Stir in sesame the seeds.

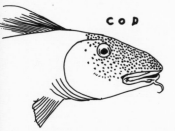

COD

dinner

dinner
miso-marinated cod
↓

lunch
chicken yakitori
↳ p. 90

To serve, plate the fish topped with the herbs and reserved whole capers, then drizzle with the sauce. Serve salted ponzu sauce on the side.

margot and fergus henderson

chicken, leek, and tarragon pie

Serves 6–8

For the chicken and chicken stock:
4–5 sprigs fresh parsley
3 bay leaves
4 sprigs fresh tarragon, stems and leaves separated*
4 leeks, trimmed and washed, 2 leeks cut into 1½-inch (4 cm) pieces, 2 diced
2 carrots, diced
1 onion, diced
1 whole free-range chicken and giblets
½ bottle (375 ml) white wine
1 tablespoon black peppercorns

For the pie:
1 14 oz (400 g) package frozen puff pastry
5 tablespoons (70 g) unsalted butter
½ cup (70 g) all-purpose (plain) flour
⅔ cup (5 fl oz/150 ml) Madeira or white wine
1 tablespoon Dijon mustard
2 tablespoons capers
⅔ cup (5 fl oz/150 ml) crème fraîche
Grated zest of ½ lemon
1½ cups (12 fl oz/350 ml) chicken stock
salt and freshly ground black pepper
1 egg, whisked

Our kids—a son, Hector, and two daughters, Owen and Frances—grew up in restaurants. We taught them to suck the heads of a langoustine at a very young age. They were quite proud of that. Of course, they still ate a lot of tomato pasta, baked potatoes, cheese on toast. It wasn't all glamorous, but they loved their food. Greens were a little harder to get into them, but this pie is a very unctuous and gentle giving dish. It's soothing and the greens are tucked under a crispy top. The chicken can be poached the day before. In fact, it can even benefit from being cooked beforehand. But don't forget to take the pastry out of the freezer! It's a bore to get through it all and find your pastry is rock hard. This is a dish I [Margot] used to make for dinner back when the kids were quite young, when I was balancing being in the kitchen and being a mom. Frequently Fergus would come home after the kids had eaten but would cook another meal just because he wanted to. He's quite good at making faces with food, frankfurters with curly hair and ketchup, that sort of thing. The dough work face is his touch. Serve this with either mashed potatoes, rutabaga (swede), or new potatoes and hispi (pointed) cabbage.

•

Make the chicken and chicken stock:
Tie together the parsley stems, bay leaves, and tarragon stems.

In a pot large enough to contain the chicken easily with the vegetables and water, make a bed at the bottom of the pot by spreading out the diced leeks, carrots, and onion, plus the bundled herbs. Snuggle the chicken into the vegetables and add the giblets.

Add water to cover the chicken entirely and bring to a boil over medium-high heat. Adjust the heat to low and simmer for 8 minutes. Add the larger pieces of leek and simmer for 2 additional minutes. Scoop out the large pieces of leek and

⌂ ST. JOHN, ROCHELLE
CANTEEN (LONDON, UK)
•
☺ HECTOR, 26; OWEN,
21; FRANCES, 21

dinner
chicken, leek,
and tarragon pie
↓

treats
blood orange upside
down cake
↳ p. 196

set aside for the pie. Remove the pot from the heat, put the lid on, and leave to completely cool.

Make the pie:
At least 40 minutes before preparing, remove the puff pastry from the freezer to thaw.

Preheat the oven to 350°F (180°C/Gas Mark 4).

In a heavy-bottomed pan, melt the butter over medium heat. Add the flour, stirring with a wooden spoon or whisk until incorporated. Cook the roux for 5 minutes.

Add the Madeira and cook for 3–4 more minutes, stirring constantly. Add the mustard, capers, crème fraîche, and lemon zest, stirring until incorporated. Slowly whisk in the chicken stock, whisking all the time, so as not to get lumps. Season well with salt and black pepper.

Tear the chicken into 1-inch (2.5 cm) pieces and add this to the sauce along with the reserved leeks and tarragon leaves. Season with salt and black pepper again if needed.

Pour the mixture into an 8 × 11-inch (20 × 28 cm) baking dish.

Roll out the puff pastry on a well-floured surface until it is slightly larger than the size of the baking dish. Brush the edges of the baking dish with beaten egg. Gently lay the pastry on top, crimping the edges, then egg wash the whole pie.

Bake until golden brown, 15–20 minutes.

* Pick the leaves off the tarragon sprigs. Use the stems for the stock and the leaves for the sauce.

roast chicken
with artichoke salad

Serves 4

For the chicken:
1 whole chicken
Salt and freshly ground black pepper
½ lemon
⅔ cup (150 g) unsalted butter
1 sprig fresh rosemary
1 sprig fresh thyme
1 oz (20 g) minced garlic

For the salad:
1 large onion, diced
1 head of iceberg lettuce, washed and roughly chopped
20 cherry tomatoes, halved
4 marinated artichoke hearts, halved
4 hard-boiled eggs, quartered
Extra-virgin olive oil
Sea salt and freshly ground black pepper
1 teaspoon Chardonnay vinegar
2 tablespoons roasted pine nuts
3½ oz (100 g) Parmesan cheese
3½ oz (100 g) croutons
Generous ⅓ cup (3½ fl oz/100 ml) yogurt dressing

Equipment
Kamado-style grill

Sandra and I [Filip] started De Jonkman fourteen years ago, the month after Fleur was born. We've led a hectic life since. But we spend every Sunday with the family and kids. We live outside the city, five kilometers from the restaurant, surrounded by fields and woods. When it's nice out, we never go inside. This recipe comes from Sandra's childhood. When she was a little girl, she lived in a small town called Veurne on the French border. Every Sunday she and her parents would buy a roasted chicken at the market and prepare it at home with potatoes and this classic artichoke salad. We love to continue the tradition at home. I grill while Sandra prepares the salad and the kids play outside.

•

Cook the chicken:
Season the chicken inside and out by rubbing with pepper, salt, lemon, butter, rosemary, thyme, and garlic. Preheat a kamado-style grill to 400°F (200°C/Gas Mark 6). (Alternatively you can simply roast the chicken at 350°F (175°C/Gas Mark 4) for 1½ hours. Place the chicken in a casserole, transfer to the grill, and let it cook for 1 hour. Remove and let rest before carving.

Assemble the salad:
In a large bowl, combine the onion, lettuce, tomatoes, artichokes, and eggs and dress with some olive oil, sea salt, and black pepper. Give it some more flavor with Chardonnay vinegar. Add some roasted pine nuts. Finish with thin slices of Parmesan cheese and the croutons. You can add the dressing on top of the salad. (But our kids like this even more with mayonnaise or ketchup.)

Serve the chicken alongside the salad.

⌂ **RESTAURANT DE JONKMAN (BRUGES, BELGIUM)**
•
☺ **FLEUR, 14; JULES, 9**

<u>dinner</u>
roast chicken
with artichoke salad
↓

<u>treats</u>
daddy's crêpes normandy
↳ p. 202

roast chicken with noodles

Serves 4

1 medium cucumber
¼ cup (50 g) sugar
Scant ¼ cup (50 ml) vinegar
1 small free-range good-quality chicken
1 teaspoon cooking oil
½ teaspoon salt
14½ oz (410 g) fresh egg noodles
1 tablespoon peanut butter
½ teaspoon soy sauce
½ teaspoon sesame seeds

Sunday meals have always been important to us, as it is our rare day off. And nothing is more traditional than a Sunday roast. This version nods toward Malaysia with the egg noodles and to Chinese cold noodles. We've found our daughter loves the combination of soy sauce and sesame seeds. And noodles. Basically Shea eats anything with noodles. What's nice for us is that we can prepare the dish for her with just a little less spice and then add some for ourselves and sit down to a family dinner, all eating (a version of) the same thing.

•

Peel, then cut the cucumber into sticks 2 inches (5 cm) long, easy for the baby to pick up and manage. Place the cucumber in a heatproof bowl.

In a small saucepan, bring the sugar, vinegar, and a scant ¼ cup (50 ml) water to a boil. Allow to cool, then pour over the cucumber and let sit for a minimum of 2 hours. (Whatever you don't use will last 1 month refrigerated in an airtight container.)

Meanwhile, preheat the oven to 425°F (220°C/Gas Mark 7).

Rub the chicken with the oil and salt and roast until nice and golden, about 20 minutes. Reduce the oven temperature to 350°F (180°C/Gas Mark 4) and cook for a further 40 minutes until the juices run clear.

Remove the chicken from the oven, cover with foil, and cool to room temperature. Pick off all the cooked chicken into small pieces. (Save the carcass for a yummy stock.)

<u>dinner</u>
roast chicken
with noodles
↓

<u>snacks</u>
pork and zucchini
dumplings
↳ p. 118

Place the egg noodles in a heatproof bowl and pour boiling water over them. Allow to stand for around 4 minutes, then drain. In a bowl, whisk together the peanut butter, soy, and sesame seeds, add the still-warm noodles, and mix well.

Now put the noodles in the little nipper's bowl, top with some of the chicken, and serve with cucumber sticks.

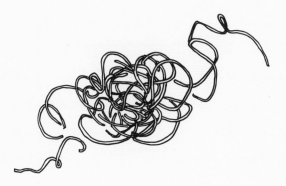

james knappett and sandia chang

stuffed cabbage with potatoes, shallots, and mustard sauce

heinz reitbauer

For the pork stuffing:
1 lb (475 g) lean pork, cut into ⅓-inch (1 cm) dice
4 oz (115 g) pork fatback, cut into ⅓-inch (1 cm) dice
1½ oz (45 g) lardo or German speck, cut into ⅓-inch (1 cm) dice
5 tablespoons (75 g) unsalted butter
7½ oz (215 g) onions, finely chopped
1 oz (30 g) garlic, finely chopped
1 teaspoon (2 g) coriander seeds, toasted and crushed
½ teaspoon (2 g) mustard seeds, toasted and crushed
1 teaspoon (2 g) cayenne pepper
1 teaspoon sweet paprika
½ roll, soaked in milk then squeezed dry
2 oz (50 g) Topaz apple or similar tart apple
3½ oz (100 g) Carpathian salt
1½ oz (45 g) prune, brunoised
2 tablespoons fresh lovage, minced
2 tablespoons fresh chervil, minced
1 tablespoon fresh marjoram, minced
Freshly ground black pepper

For the cabbage:
1 large head green cabbage, outer leaves and stem trimmed
Salt
2 cloves fermented black garlic
2 dried prunes
4 pieces pork caul fat, well washed
3¼ cups (25 fl oz/750 ml) beef stock
20 new potatoes
15 griselle (grey) shallots, minced
5 sprigs fresh thyme

For the mustard-caper sauce:
1 teaspoon cornstarch (cornflour)
2 teaspoons stone-ground mustard
3 tablespoons Dijon mustard
3 tablespoons capers, finely chopped

During most of the year, I am extremely short on time to cook at home. But in the summer, the whole family heads to our hut in the mountains, with little electricity and no cell phone service. There I love to cook all day long for my family. Even though we're only there for one week at a time, the mountains give me the necessary peace and tranquility to last a year. Among our favorites is this heartwarming and comforting dinner, featuring the sweetness of griselle shallots and the heartiness of stuffed cabbage. The meal is tasty and delicious, our family's soul food.

●

Prepare the pork stuffing:
In a bowl set over a larger bowl with crushed ice, combine the diced pork, fatback, and lardo.

In a saucepan, melt the butter over medium heat. Add the onions, garlic, coriander, mustard seeds, cayenne, and paprika and caramelize, about 10 minutes. Then put the pan on ice to let the ingredients cool down.

Mince together the chilled meat, garlic/onion mixture, roll, apple, and salt. Add the prune, lovage, chervil, and marjoram. Season with pepper to taste. Cover with foil and put on crushed ice.

Prepare the cabbage:
Bring a pot of salted water to a boil.

Carefully remove one cabbage leaf after the other until the heart of the cabbage is left. Blanch the leaves for 10 seconds in the boiling water. Blanch the heart of the cabbage for about 2 minutes. Dry off on a tea towel.

Take the heart of the cabbage and put it in the center of a plate. Set aside the 4 largest leaves. Then take 1 leaf

⌂ STEIRERECK
IM STADTPARK
(VIENNA, AUSTRIA)
•
☺ LORENZ, 16;
CHARLOTTE, 14; LOUISA, 5

dinner
stuffed cabbage with
potatoes, shallots,
and mustard sauce
↓

treats
hazelnut puddings
with raspberry sauce
↳ p. 220

of cabbage after the other and spread 2 tablespoons of the
pork stuffing on each cabbage leaf, allowing the edges to
remain free. Put one after the other around the cabbage heart,
reassembling the head of cabbage until it is "whole" again.

Slice the fermented garlic and prunes and place atop
the stuffed cabbage head, then cover with the 4 reserved
large cabbage leaves. Cover the stuffed cabbage head
with the caul fat and refrigerate to allow the ingredients
to cool and firm up.

Preheat the oven to 350°F (180°C/Gas Mark 4).

In a Dutch oven (casserole), heat the beef stock until
simmering. Set the stuffed cabbage stem-side down in
the pot. Add the potatoes, shallots, and thyme. Cover,
transfer to the oven, and oven-braise for 1 hour.

Uncover and continue to bake until golden brown, an
additional 3–5 minutes. Remove the pan from the oven
and let rest for 3–5 minutes. Remove the cabbage while
reserving the braising liquid.

Make the mustard-caper sauce:
Put 2 cups (16 fl oz/475 ml) of the braising liquid in a small
bowl. Add the cornstarch (cornflour) to the reserved braising
liquid to thicken. Once incorporated, add the mustards,
stirring well, and then the capers. Mix until well incorporated.

To serve, cut the cabbage open like a cake. Serve with the
new potatoes, shallots, and mustard-caper sauce.

heinz reitbauer

claudette zepeda-wilkins

albondigas-inspired meatloaf

Serves 6–8

For the chipotle sauce:
2 tablespoons olive oil
1 medium yellow onion, julienned
2 cloves garlic, minced
22 oz (625 g) tomatoes (beefsteak or heirloom), diced
1 tablespoon tomato paste (purée)
1 can (7 oz/198 g) chipotle peppers in adobo sauce
½ cup (4 fl oz/120 ml) beef or chicken stock
5 fresh mint leaves
2 sprigs fresh oregano
2 sprigs fresh marjoram
Salt and freshly ground black pepper
½ cup (15 g) fresh cilantro sprigs (coriander), minced
½ cup (15 g) Italian parsley sprigs, minced

For the meatloaf:
2 slices stale bread
¼ cup (2 fl oz/60 ml) whole milk
1 lb (455 g) ground (minced) pork
1 lb (455 g) ground (minced) beef
2 eggs
⅔ cup (5 fl oz/150 ml) Worcestershire sauce
2 cloves garlic, minced
4 tablespoons soaked jasmine rice
Salt and freshly ground black pepper
4 soft-boiled eggs, peeled

"

Eating and cooking at home has definitely been something I have worked on prioritizing for my kids the last few years. Early in my career it was incredibly difficult to do with my schedule. Now cooking at home is simple and we do it together to make light work of it. We usually talk on Sunday about what we feel like eating in the week and shop/prep for that.

"

I am a first-generation Mexican-American with biracial children. Their tastes are not those I grew up with. For instance, I never had meatloaf, a touchstone of the American kitchen. But I did grow up eating what, in my opinion, are the best *albóndigas al chipotle* that my mother made. *Albóndigas* are Mexican meatballs, often served in a soup (*sopa di albóndigas*) but also accompanied with this chipotle sauce rich with herbs and spices. This hybrid recipe encapsulates both traditions—American and Mexican—in a way I hope my kids will carry with them into the future.

•

Make the chipotle sauce:
In a heavy-bottomed sauté pan, heat the olive oil over medium heat until shimmering. Add the onion and garlic and cook, stirring as needed, until the onions are golden (careful not to burn the garlic), approximately 7 minutes. Add the tomatoes, tomato paste (purée), chipotle peppers, stock, mint, oregano, and marjoram. Cook until the sauce thickens and reduces by 30 percent, 20–25 minutes. Remove from the heat and season with salt and black pepper to taste.

Discard the herb sprigs, transfer the sauce to a food processor or blender, and pulse 3–4 times until roughly chopped. Let cool to room temperature, then stir in the cilantro (coriander) and parsley.

Make the meatloaf:
Preheat the oven to 350°F (180°C/Gas Mark 4).

Break up the stale bread into small pieces, place in a bowl, and pour the milk over to soak. Set aside.

dinner
albondigas-inspired
meatloaf
↓

breakfast
claudette's famous
french toast
↳ p. 38

In a large bowl, mix together the two ground (minced) meats. Add 1 cup (8 fl oz/250 ml) of the chipotle sauce, the fresh eggs, Worcestershire sauce, garlic, and rice. Season with salt and pepper. Squeeze the bread to remove excess milk, then add it to the meat. Mix until well incorporated.

Fill an 8½ × 4½-inch (21.5 × 11.5 cm) loaf pan with half the meat mixture. Nestle in the whole soft-boiled eggs, then cover with the remaining mix. Top with ½ cup (4 fl oz/120 ml) of the chipotle sauce.

Transfer to the oven and bake for 45 minutes. Rotate the pan front to back and bake until the juices run clear and the rice has fully cooked, another 45 minutes to 1 hour.

To serve, either spread the remaining chipotle sauce on top or serve on the side.

karena armstrong

roasted lamb shoulder, bao, and pickles

Serves 5

For the lamb:
2½ teaspoons (10 g) fenugreek seeds
4½ teaspoons (10 g) cumin seeds
5 tablespoons (40 g) flaky sea salt
4½ teaspoons (10 g) smoked paprika
2 teaspoons (5 g) ground white pepper
3 tablespoons plus 1 teaspoon (50 ml) rice bran oil or similar neutral oil
1 boneless lamb shoulder (about 4 lb/1.8 kg)
1 large yellow onion, sliced
8 cloves garlic, sliced
1 oz (30 g) fresh ginger, sliced
1 bunch cilantro (coriander), roots only, sliced
About 2 cups (16 fl oz/475 ml) chicken stock

For the pickles:
⅔ cup (5 fl oz/150 ml) distilled white vinegar
1½ tablespoons (20 g) sugar
1 teaspoon (5 g) sea salt
Aromatics including bay leaves/cinnamon/chili
4 large carrots, sliced
1 bunch radishes, sliced
1 small red onion, sliced
1 English (seedless) cucumber, sliced

My boys love this meal because there's an element of do-it-yourself. Plus, with a family as busy as ours, it's great because we always have pickles in the fridge. More recently, now that Fletcher's almost a teenager, I've also recruited the boys to help with prep and cleanup. I figure if they're old enough to work a computer they can peel a carrot, too. This makes enough for us to use the lamb shoulder as leftovers in the following days.

•

Prepare the lamb:
Preheat the oven to 275°F (135°C/Gas Mark 1).

In a small fry frying pan, combine the fenugreek and cumin and toast gently until aromatic. Remove from the heat and grind in a spice grinder with the salt. Combine with the paprika and white pepper and then whisk together the spices with the rice bran oil. Rub the lamb all over with the spice mix, then put the lamb in a roasting pan that is a snug fit.

Add the onion, garlic, ginger, and cilantro (coriander) roots to the roasting pan. Add enough stock to come just one-quarter of the way up the lamb. Depending on the size of your pan, you may not need all the stock listed.

Cover the lamb with parchment paper and then foil and wrap it very tightly. Transfer to the oven and slow-cook the lamb until tender but not falling apart, for approximately 4 hours.

Remove the paper and foil from the lamb and increase the oven temperature to 425°F (220°C/Gas Mark 7). Return to the oven and roast for 20 minutes to crisp the fat layer until golden brown.

Make the pickles:
In a small saucepan, combine the vinegar, sugar, ⅔ cup (5 fl oz/150 ml) water, salt, and aromatics and bring to a boil. Simmer for 5 minutes to dissolve the sugar. Cool before use.

LAMB BAD

BAA BAAO

⌂ THE SALOPIAN INN
(MCLAREN VALE,
AUSTRALIA)
•
☺ HARRY, 14;
SEBASTIAN, 12;
FLETCHER, 10

dinner
roasted lamb
shoulder, bao,
and pickles
↓

lunch
lunch box noodle bowl
⌙ p. 78

For the coconut hoisin sauce:
½ cup (150 g) hoisin sauce
¾ cup (150 g) coconut cream
3 tablespoons plus 1 teaspoon (50 ml)
fresh lime juice

For the steamed bao:
2½ cups (320 g) bread flour (strong
white flour)
7½ tablespoons (70 g) superfine
(caster) sugar
6½ teaspoons (20 g) instant dry yeast
5 teaspoons vegetable oil
4 teaspoons (20 g) baking powder

For serving:
1 bunch cilantro (coriander), trimmed
and washed
1 bunch scallions (spring onions),
trimmed and washed
1 head butter lettuce, separated into
leaves

Equipment
Tiered Chinese steamer

"

The boys have only ever known real
food. We always have a few choices
of plant foods and don't make a big
fuss really, but what is for dinner or
the meal is all there is, so if you don't
eat, you're hungry. With three boys
that is quite a motivator.

"

Put the carrots, radishes, onion, and cucumber in separate
containers. Pour over some of the pickling liquid. (These
pickles can be made well in advance and keep for months
in your refrigerator.)

Make the coconut hoisin sauce:
In a bowl, stir together the hoisin, coconut cream, and lime
juice. Refrigerate until needed

Make the bao:
In a stand mixer fitted with the dough hook, combine the flour,
sugar, yeast, ¾ cup plus 1 tablespoon (7 fl oz/200 ml) water,
and oil. Mix and knead the dough for 10 minutes, or until
cohesive and sticky. Cover and allow the dough to double in
size, approximately 1 hour.

Cut out 20 rectangles (1¼ × 2½ inches/3 × 6 cm) of
parchment paper.

Add the baking powder to the dough and mix in well. Divide the
dough into 20 balls. Flatten each ball of dough and roll into a
small rectangle about ⅓-inch (8 mm) thick. Fold the dough over
the rectangle of parchment paper (this prevents the two sides
of the bao from sticking), then fold the overhang of the paper
under the base. The paper is shaped like an S. Arrange the bao
in a Chinese steamer basket so they are not touching.

Set up a pan of simmering water. Set the steamer on top and
steam the bao for 6 minutes. Cool if not using immediately.

To serve:
Slice the lamb. Set out the meat, pickles, cilantro, scallions
(spring onions), lettuce leaves, and coconut hoisin sauce. Set
out the bao (reheated if they were made in advance) and let
the family construct, placing the lamb, pickles, leaves, herbs,
and sauce inside the bao.

karena armstrong

lamb curry

Serves 6

1 head garlic, peeled
6 red shallots, peeled
1 inch (2.5 cm) fresh ginger, peeled
1 bunch of cilantro (coriander) roots
½ cup (4 fl oz/120 ml) non-GMO canola (rapeseed) oil
3½ tablespoons curry powder
2 tablespoons garam masala
1 tablespoon cumin seeds
1 tablespoon fennel seeds
3 bay leaves
½ teaspoon ground cinnamon
¼ teaspoon freshly ground black pepper
1 tablespoon palm sugar
4 tablespoons fish sauce
6 lb 10 oz (3 kg) lamb shoulder, cut into 2-inch (5 cm) pieces
Salt
2¼ lb (1 kg) waxy potatoes, peeled and cut into 2-inch (5 cm) chunks
1 cup (230 g) plain (natural) yogurt
Generous ¾ cup (200 g) coconut yogurt
1⅔ cups (400 g) strained tomatoes (passata)
2 tablespoons tomato paste (tomato purée)

This curry is a hybrid of many influences, from deep studies of Thai cookery in my late teens and early twenties to years spent cooking alongside Sunny Sharmam, a beloved former Attica staff member who hails from Waraich in Amritsar, Punjab. My kids love curry, and this is a mellow recipe acknowledging their developing taste buds. We often serve it with steamed brown basmati rice, a coconut relish, and myriad green vegetables, as curry is an excellent way to increase children's consumption of healthy foods! To make the recipe vegetarian, either forgo the lamb entirely or replace with eggplant or tofu.

•

In a food processor or blender, pulse the garlic, shallots, ginger, and cilantro (coriander) roots into a paste.

In a large heavy-bottomed saucepan, combine the herb paste and canola (rapeseed) oil and cook over a gentle heat until fragrant and the raw onion smell has disappeared, about 10 minutes.

Add the curry powder, garam masala, cumin, fennel, bay leaves, cinnamon, and black pepper and cook for 3 minutes longer. Add the palm sugar, stir well, and fry until caramelized, about 2 minutes. Reduce the heat, add the fish sauce, and cook for 30 seconds.

Add the lamb and salt to taste and mix well, making sure the spices coat the lamb pieces on all sides. Stir in the potatoes and similarly coat. Stir in both yogurts, the strained tomatoes (passata), and tomato paste (tomato purée). Simmer until the lamb is tender, about 1½ hours.

Check the seasoning, adding more salt more if necessary. Let rest covered for a couple of hours in the refrigerator so that the flavors can deepen. Reheat to serve.

icelandic fish stew with rye bread

Serves 6

For the sweet rye bread:
7¾ cups (800 g) rye flour
3⅓ cups (400 g) whole wheat (wholemeal) flour
9 tablespoons (200 g) golden syrup
4 teaspoons baking soda (bicarbonate of soda)
2 teaspoons salt
4¼ cups (34 fl oz/1 liter) buttermilk

For the fish stew:
3½ tablespoons (50 g) unsalted butter
1 white onion, thinly sliced
¼ teaspoon grated nutmeg
Salt and freshly ground pepper
2 tablespoons all-purpose (plain) flour
1¼ cups (10 fl oz/300 ml) whole milk
1 lb (500 g) small potatoes, peeled
3–4 fresh bay leaves
9 oz (250 g) cod
7 oz (200 g) smoked haddock
½ oz (10 g) fresh horseradish, grated

For serving:
Salt
7 oz (200 g) rutabaga (swede), cut into small pieces
½ tablespoon (8 g) butter
2 oz (50 g) sorrel, whole and rinsed
Butter, for the bread

This is a spin on a very traditional Icelandic dish called *plokkfiskur*, which everyone in Iceland loves. The potato-and-fish stew is the definition of comfort food and is a very good introduction to fish dishes for kids who are afraid to try fish. It basically looks just like mashed potatoes, to which most kids can relate. I use fresh fish—cod and haddock—but it's also a great way to use leftovers.

•

Make the rye bread:
Arrange racks in the lower and center positions of the oven and preheat the oven to 250°F (120°C/Gas Mark ½).

In a large bowl, combine both flours, the syrup, baking soda (bicarb), salt, and buttermilk. Mix together until a dough is formed. Place the dough in a 9 × 5-inch (23 × 12.5 cm) loaf pan. Place a pan of water on the lower rack and place the bread on the center rack. Slow-bake for 4 hours 30 minutes. Turn off the oven and let it rest in the oven for another 4 hours 30 minutes or so before serving.

Make the fish stew:
Preheat the oven to 400°F (200°C/Gas Mark 6.)

In a heavy-bottomed skillet, heat the butter over low heat. Add the onion and nutmeg, season with salt and pepper, and cook until the onions soften. Stir in the flour, then the milk. Whisk together to create a chunky béchamel.

Bring a large pot of salted water to a boil. Add the potatoes and bay leaves and cook until tender, approximately 20 minutes. Drain and then mash. Stir into the béchamel.

Meanwhile, arrange the cod and smoked haddock on a sheet pan and bake until opaque, about 10 minutes.

⌂ SLIPPURINN
(VESTMANNAEYJABÆR,
ICELAND)
•
☺ ÁSTÞÓR, 12; ODDNÝ, 9;
EMILÍA, 3; AUÐUNN, 1

dinner
icelandic fish stew
with rye bread
↓

treats
twisted doughnut,
cardamom sugar,
and caramel
↳ p. 224

Mash the fish into the béchamel-potato mixture. Season
with the horseradish and salt and, aggressively, with pepper.
The dish should be quite high in pepper.

To serve:
Bring a pot of salted water to a boil. Add the rutabaga (swede)
and cook until tender, about 10 minutes. Remove and toss
with some salt and the butter.

Equally divide the stew among six bowls. Serve alongside
rutabaga, fresh sorrel, and slices of rye bread, spread with
a very generous amount of butter.

jp mcmahon

whole baked turbot with mussels and buttered greens

Serves 4

1 whole turbot (about 9 lb/4 kg), gutted
Cold-pressed canola (rapeseed) oil
Sea salt
2 leeks, halved lengthwise
7 tablespoons (100 g) unsalted butter, cubed
2 cups (16 fl oz/475 ml) fish stock
1 lb (455 g) mussels, scrubbed and debearded
Handful of fresh fennel fronds

🌾 ⓧ

I love fish, but trying to get my kids to love it as much as I do has been a challenge at times. Preparing whole fish though is a start. It's a simple and fast technique and, by starting with the fish in its entirety, it's a great way to educate them about its anatomy too. Here I use a turbot but you can do the same dish with any whole flatfish. In terms of vegetables, I must admit, they don't always eat the greens, but at least they eat broccoli. Though they do accuse me of not cooking it enough, saying that it's too hard and you can't suck it!

•

Preheat the oven to 400°F (200°C/Gas Mark 6).

Trim the turbot of its fins and tail. Oil the top and bottom of the fish and season with sea salt.

Place the leeks in the bottom of a large roasting pan and dress with a little oil and the butter and season with sea salt. Pour the fish stock over the leeks. Lay the fish on top of the leeks.

Roast until the internal temperature of the fish reaches 130°F (55°C), about 20 minutes. For the last 2–3 minutes add the mussels.

Remove the fish from the oven. Discard any mussels that have not opened. Baste the fish and mussels with the sauce. Top with fresh fennel fronds.

TURBO TURBOT

dinner

<u>dinner</u>
whole baked turbot
with mussels
and buttered greens
↓

<u>lunch</u>
pasta with butter
and parmesan
↳ p. 86

NICE
MUSSELS!

max strohe and ilona scholl

scallop, carrot, and brown butter

Serves 4

For the scallops:
20 in-shell scallops

For the scallop broth:
Vegetable oil
5 carrots, diced
½ stalk celery, diced
3 onions, diced
2 leeks, white parts only, diced
11 lb (5 kg) mussel meats
Half of a 28-oz (800 g) can tomato paste (purée)
6¼ cups (50 fl oz/1.5 liters) red wine
Scallop trimmings*
2 cups (16 fl oz/475 ml) fish stock
1 egg white

For the carrot purée:
3 tablespoons (45 g) unsalted butter
2¼ lb (1 kg) carrots, grated
1¼ cups (10 fl oz/300 ml) carrot juice
2 cups (16 fl oz/475 ml) heavy (whipping) cream
Salt

For serving:
4 teaspoons clarified butter
Flaky sea salt

This is a kid-friendly variation of a dish we do at the restaurant. Mimi is a chef's child. Her second living room is—as is ours—the restaurant. She helps, teases, and pranks us, plays under the tables, does her homework, and has staff food with us. Sometimes, when she is in the kitchen in the first hours of service, she does the dishes (precleaning some pots using her tongue and fingers, especially the dessert ones). She is very curious about the plates that leave the kitchen, and the ones we can let her try, she tries. The scallop is one of our signatures. Normally there are a few more elements, but we've removed them to Mimi's taste. We've removed the XO sauce since she says it's too spicy; the sea urchin because she doesn't like it; and the decorative flowers, which she does not care for. But the nonspicy, reduced variation of the scallop, she absolutely adores. It is our way of showing her that when extraordinary product quality meets the passion, experience, and creativity of a kitchen team, you'll have a "Mmmm" moment ahead of you.

•

Prepare the scallops:
Crack open the fresh scallops and cut the adductor muscles out of their shells. Pull off the little side muscle from the scallops. Save all the other trimmings* for the stock. Refrigerate the scallops while you reduce the broth.

Make the scallop broth:
Cover the bottom of a soup pot with a thin layer of vegetable oil over high heat. Add the carrots and celery and sauté until they take on color. Reduce the heat, add the onions and leeks and cook until caramelized, about 10 minutes. Please keep in mind that the bottom of the pot should always be covered in a layer of vegetable oil. Add some, if necessary.

Add the mussels and the tomato paste (purée) and also let it caramelize. Add one-third of the wine, let it simmer until reduced by half, and repeat until the wine is gone.

⌂ TULUS LOTREK
(BERLIN, GERMANY)
•
☺ EMILIA (MIMI), 10

dinner
scallop, carrot,
and brown butter
↓

snacks
leek, cream,
and stinking stones
↳ p. 112

Add the fish stock and bring to a boil. Reduce to a simmer and cook for 2½ hours. If it begins to burn, add water or fish stock. Strain and return to the pot to cool down. Add the scallop trimmings and egg white and simmer for 1 more hour. Strain carefully through a cloth and reduce again. The consistency should resemble soy sauce: thin but with an intense flavor.

Make the carrot purée:
In a large flat-bottomed pot, melt the butter over medium heat. Add the carrots and braise until soft, approximately 25 minutes. Add the carrot juice and cook over low heat until the carrots are soft and most of the liquid has evaporated. Add the cream and bring to a simmer. Once simmering, purée with a hand blender until smooth. Season with salt to taste.

To serve:
In a frying pan, heat the clarified butter over medium heat. Add the scallops and cook until the outside of the scallop gets a bit toasty, but the inside is still "glassy," not completely cooked through.

Slices the scallops horizontally into 3 slices and put some sea salt flakes on top.

Place 1 tablespoon of the carrot purée in each of four bowls. Pour some of the broth over it, and place the scallops on top. You only need a spoon to eat this and you always have the perfect balance of scallop, purée, and broth. Let yourself be celebrated by the kids.

* Save all the innards and other pieces trimmed off the scallop shells and throw them into the stock. This stuff that usually gets thrown away has a lot of flavor.

ARE YOU A SCALLOP?
NO, I'M A FAN.
OH, THANKS!
UM...

jock zonfrillo

hot and sour fried kangaroo tail

Serves 4

For the kangaroo tail:
Grapeseed oil, for browning
4½ lb (2 kg) kangaroo tails, cut
into sections
Salt and freshly ground black pepper
10½ oz (300 g) yellow onions, diced
6 tablespoons (100 g) tomato
paste (purée)
¼ teaspoon (5 g) fresh lemon
myrtle leaves
¼ teaspoon (5 g) fresh aniseed
myrtle leaves
¼ teaspoon (5 g) fresh cinnamon
myrtle leaves
¼ teaspoon (5 g) fresh Geraldton wax
⅛ teaspoon (2 g) fresh native thyme
¼ teaspoon (5 g) fresh
mountain pepper
8½ tablespoons (60 g) Dorrigo dried
pepper berries, or black peppercorns,
freshly ground
1 oz (30 g) garlic, roughly chopped
7 oz (200 g) native tamarind
⅓ cup (100 g) palm sugar
1¼ cups (10 fl oz/300 ml) kangaroo or
beef stock
⅓ cup plus 1 tablespoon (3½ fl oz/
100 ml) shoyu
2 tablespoons (30 ml) abalone
fish sauce
1 lb (455 g) Kestrel potatoes,
unpeeled, quartered
10½ oz (300 g) carrots, cut into
1.5-inch (4 cm) chunks

For the carrot frying:
1¼ cups (200 g) rice flour
1¼ cups (200 g) potato flour
7 tablespoons (50 g) dried Dorrigo
pepper berries, or black peppercorns,
freshly ground
1½ teaspoons salt
Grapeseed oil, for deep-frying

Almost all children love fried chicken or, let's be honest, anything fried! Using that as a vehicle, this recipe is also an introduction to Indigenous Australian ingredients and spices. It has been super popular in our house: the end result has a real taste of Australia through the spices as well as being fried crispy, a little bit spicy, and finally sour and tangy. All the things kids go wild for! More important, with this one recipe I can teach my children how to caramelize meat properly, how to braise meat on the bone, how to create a balanced sauce with the five tastes—sweet, salty, sour, bitter, and umami. All that is required in addition to this is some green vegetables and steamed rice for a perfect dinner.

•

Make the kangaroo tail:
In a heavy-bottomed pan, heat a splash of oil over medium-high heat. Season one side of the roo tails generously with salt and black pepper. Add the larger pieces of tails to the pan and brown each side. While one side is browning, season the other side with more salt and black pepper.

Set aside the browned roo tail. Add the onions and sauté for 2 minutes. Add the tomato paste (purée) and all the herbs and spices and sauté for another 3 minutes. Add the garlic and sauté for 1 more minute, until the pan starts catching on the bottom.

Add the tamarind and palm sugar and scrape the bottom of the pan well. Cook for another 2 minutes, until the pan starts catching again. Add the stock and deglaze by scrubbing all the flavorful browned bits off the bottom of the pot with a wooden spoon.

Finally, add the shoyu, fish sauce, potatoes, carrots, and browned roo tails. Transfer everything to a pressure cooker, seal, and cook at high pressure for 45 minutes. Then quick-release the pressure.

🏠 **RESTAURANT ORANA (ADELAIDE, AUSTRALIA)**

•

☺ AVA, 20; SOFIA, 15; ALFIE, 3

dinner
hot and sour fried kangaroo tail

↓

treats
paperbark ice cream and macadamia wafers

↳ p. 218

Remove the roo tails and let cool to room temperature in the sauce. (It is critical they be allowed to cool to room temperature in the sauce.) When cool, remove the roo tail pieces and refrigerate for at least 2 hours so they can firm up. Meanwhile, pass the sauce through a fine-mesh sieve and transfer to a saucepan. Reduce the sauce until really thick, then balance the seasoning with more shoyu, native tamarind, and mountain pepper. Discard the solids and set aside.

Fry the roo tails:
Bring the roo tails to room temperature.

In a shallow bowl, mix both flours, the pepper, and salt together. In a second shallow bowl, stir 3 tablespoons water into ½ cup (100 g) of the braising sauce. Pass the roo tail through the liquid, then into the flour mixture and let sit for 1 hour.

Repeat the process above and let sit for at least another 30 minutes.

Pour 3 inches (7.5 cm) grapeseed oil into a large deep pot and heat to 350°F (180°C). Working in batches, add the coated roo tails to the hot oil and fry until golden brown. Remove from the oil to a heatproof bowl and immediately toss together with the reserved sauce and more ground pepper to your taste, and serve.

KANGAROO TAILS

mickael viljanen

braised cheek of beef, leftover bread, pickles, and mashed potatoes

Serves 4

For the beef cheeks:
4 beef cheeks (12–14 oz/350–400 g each), trimmed clean
Salt and freshly ground pepper
½ cup (65 g) all-purpose (plain) flour
Neutral oil, for frying
2 oz (50 g) smoked bacon, cubed
2 medium onions, diced
4 cloves garlic, crushed
Small bunch of fresh thyme
8 ½ cups (68 fl oz/2 liters) beef stock

For the garlic-fried bread:
4 cloves garlic, peeled
Pinch of sea salt
2 tablespoons (30 g) salted butter
2 tablespoons (30 g) olive oil
3½ oz (100 g) stale bread, torn into smallish pieces

For the dill pickles:
2 cucumbers, thinly sliced
Salt
1¼ cups (10 fl oz/300 ml) white wine vinegar
1 cup (200 g) sugar
1 teaspoon yellow mustard seeds
Pinch of ground turmeric
1 large bunch of dill, coarsely torn

For the mashed potatoes:
2¼ lb (1 kg) baking potatoes
10½ tablespoons (150 g) cold unsalted butter
1 cup (8 fl oz/250 ml) whole milk, warmed
Salt
Freshly grated nutmeg

For serving:
Chopped fresh chives, for garnish
Chopped fresh parsley, for garnish

With four kids and a restaurant to run, it's always been important to try to stretch the meals. This beef cheek is a great example: an economical cut that yields delicious results with relatively little work. Only time is needed to turn this gelatinous cut into something extraordinary. As with many slow-cooked meats, it only gets better when reheated. The next day, it's perfect in a ragu, a sandwich, or even as a pie. You get two dinners with only one day's work.

•

Prepare the beef cheeks:
Preheat the oven to 325°F (165°C/Gas Mark 3).

Season the beef cheeks with salt and pepper and lightly dust with flour, tapping off excess.

Heat 2 tablespoons of neutral oil in a sauté pan until shimmering. Sear the beef cheeks over medium-high heat until nicely colored. Remove the cheeks and add the bacon, onions, and garlic and cook until softened, approximately 15 minutes. Return the cheeks to the pan and add the thyme.

Move the contents of the pan to a Dutch oven (casserole) or deep braising dish and cover with the beef stock. Place a round of parchment paper on top and bring to a simmer.

Cover with a lid or foil, transfer to the oven, and bake for 3 hours to 3 hours 30 minutes. Then remove the beef cheeks and set aside.

Make the fried garlic bread:
Mash the garlic and sea salt into a paste. In a large frying pan, melt the butter in the olive oil and butter and add the garlic paste. Add the bread and toss well. Keep cooking over medium heat until caramelized and golden. Tip the bread onto paper towels to drain. Season lightly with salt if desired.

<u>dinner</u>
braised cheek of beef,
leftover bread, pickles,
and mashed potatoes
↓

<u>breakfast</u>
whipped lingonberry
semolina
↳ p. 44

Make the dill pickles:
Sprinkle the cucumber slices lightly with salt and leave for
1 hour in a colander set over a bowl.

In a saucepan, combine the vinegar, sugar, 2⅓ cups (18 fl
oz/550 ml) water, mustard seeds, turmeric, and dill and
bring to a boil. Add the cucumber slices and bring back to
a gentle simmer for 30 seconds. Remove from the heat and
let the pickles cool down in the pickling liquid. Ideally let
mature for a couple of days in the refrigerator before eating.

Make the mashed potatoes:
Preheat the oven to 350°F (180°C/Gas Mark 4).

Bake the potatoes in their skins until cooked, about 45
minutes.

Remove from the oven, split the potatoes in half, and push
the potato flesh through a fine-mesh sieve using a tea towel
over your hand so as not to burn yourself. (Discard the skins.)
Add all the butter to the potato and beat rapidly with a
wooden spoon or spatula. Add half the warm milk and beat
again, followed by the rest of the milk. Beat well for 1 minute
to emulsify, then season with salt and nutmeg to taste.

WHAT,
YOU TRY DRAWING
BEEF CHEEKS!

To serve:
Reduce the cooking stock of the cheeks to a sauce
consistency and add the cheeks. Baste to warm through
and coat.

Sprinkle the top of the glazed cheeks with the garlic-fried
bread, some chopped chives and parsley (if desired),
and a few pickles. Serve alongside the beef braising stock
and mashed potatoes.

mickael viljanen

ana roš

istrian stew

Serves 4

2¼ lb (1 kg) potatoes, cut into cubes
2¼ lb (1 kg) kidney beans, soaked overnight
3 bay leaves
6½ lb (3 kg) sour turnips or sauerkraut
1 small whole clove
10 oz (300 g) smoked pork ribs
Scant ¾ cup (5 fl oz/150 ml) extra-virgin olive oil
2 oz (50 g) garlic
2½ tablespoons (20 g) all-purpose (plain) flour
4 sausages

Jota is a hearty traditional hot pot I love to make for my family. It combines the Austro-Hungarian flavors of smoked meats and sauerkraut with the Mediterranean influence of olive oil. In nearby Italy, *jota* is also called Istrian stew. It's important for me to cook traditional dishes for my family, otherwise they won't be able to pass those recipes on to their children. That is how traditions die, and without tradition we have no identity. But that doesn't also mean my children are narrow-minded in their tastes. They've been eating in a "crazy" way since they were born. Since we've traveled so much, they've been exposed to new flavors practically since birth. Now, whether it's beef testicles, snails, frogs, whatever, it means nothing. I serve them deer heart and they'll say, "Mommy, what's this?" I'll tell them and they'll take a bite with gusto. They have very open minds, the most important part of welcoming new foods.

•

Bring a large pot of water to a boil, add the potatoes, and cook until tender, about 45 minutes. Reserving the potato water, drain the potatoes and set aside to cool. Then divide into two portions and place one portion in a bowl.

Bring a separate pot of water to a boil, add the beans and bay leaves, and simmer until tender, about 45 minutes. Reserving the bean cooking liquid, drain the beans and divide into two portions. Add one half to the potatoes in the bowl and mash.

In a third pot, bring the sour turnips to a boil and cook for 15 minutes. (Skip this step if using sauerkraut.)

⌂ **HIŠA FRANKO
(KOBARID, SLOVENIA)**

●

☺ **SVIT, 17;
EVA KLARA, 16**

<u>dinner</u>
istrian stew

↓

<u>snacks</u>
frico with potatoes,
cheese, and herbs
↳ p. 130

In one large pot, combine the reserved potato and bean cooking water. Add the unmashed beans, the sour turnips, the unmashed potatoes, and the clove. Add the smoked pork ribs and simmer for 1 hour.

Meanwhile, in a frying pan, heat the olive oil and garlic over medium heat. Add the flour and cook until golden, about 5 minutes, to make a roux.

Mix everything together—the unmashed beans, the sour turnips, the unmashed potatoes (clove removed), the smoked pork ribs, the roux, and the potato/bean mash into a large pot. Stir over medium-low heat for an additional 30 minutes to thicken.

Meanwhile, cook the sausages in a pan or on a grill over high heat until done.

For serving, divide the jota among four bowls. Top each with a sausage.

JOTA

jeremy charles

moose boil-up

Serves 10–12

3 tablespoons vegetable oil
2 lb (910 g) moose shoulder/neck, diced
2 tablespoons all-purpose (plain) flour
3 medium onions, diced
2 fresh bay leaves
Small bunch of thyme
3 cloves garlic, minced
4 tablespoons margarine
2 tablespoons tomato paste (purée)
3 large carrots, diced
3 large Yukon Gold potatoes, peeled and diced
1 medium rutabaga (swede), peeled and diced
6 cups (48 fl oz/1.4 liters) moose/chicken/vegetable stock
Salt and freshly ground black pepper

Hank and Iris haven't been on moose hunts yet, but they know I go. We're very fortunate that there are a lot of moose to harvest here in Newfoundland. The animals are a big part of our culture. Hank especially is very inquisitive about it, and these conversations offer an opportunity to talk about how lucky we are to have these big and beautiful animals to eat. Not everyone, I tell him, in the world is as lucky. This stew, which we call a boil-up, is very traditional, something we can eat all year long. It makes a wonderful winter dinner or, packed in mason jars and reheated, a camp lunch on our frequent fishing trips.

•

In a large Dutch oven (casserole), heat the vegetable oil over medium-high heat until shimmering. Toss the diced moose meat in the flour to coat, then add to the pan to brown, 3–4 minutes.

Add the onions, bay leaves, thyme sprigs, garlic, tomato paste (purée), carrots, potatoes, and rutabaga (swede). Cook over medium-low heat for 5–7 minutes, until tender.

Add the stock and bring to a boil. Once boiling, reduce to a simmer, cover, and let simmer over low heat for 2 hours. Season with salt and pepper and serve.

WRONG KIND OF MOUSSE

dinner

<u>dinner</u>
moose boil-up
↓

<u>snacks</u>
parsnip and apple soup
↳ p. 114

*

Of all the foodstuffs our children devour, sugar—the basis of dessert—is the one in which their desire for it is most clearly inversely proportional to its healthiness. It is the very enemy of health. However we are all human, and therefore we crave sweetness. To deny ourselves, and our charges, sweetness is to deprive them of one of life's most sublime blessings. The trick is to treat sweets as special treats, to bracket off dessert as something notable, something occasional, something not to be expected but always greeted with delight. An early error in my own parenting career was providing my children with a sugary special treat every day after school, by which point the treat had become no longer either special or a treat. I reined it in, but it took tears and tantrums.

Deployed conservatively, a treat is the easiest way to turn a bad day around, to readjust the hue and saturation of a blue mood into a rosy one. These recipes, which embrace sweetness, fulfill that promise that the best treats offer. Though most chefs steer clear of the pastry stations in their restaurants—pastry being a world unto itself, with its own character and schedule and idiosyncrasies—at home, many embrace the world of baking. Thus we have the Hendersons' Blood Orange Upside Down Cake (page 196), Alex Atala's grandmother-in-law's curry-tinged cake (page 198) and two different types of doughnuts: one Greek, one Icelandic. Others parents like Anne-Sophie Pic return to miracles of confection with whimsical meringues (page 204) or, like Elena Arzak, a sort of after-dinner sleight-of-hand by which a cocoa-dusted apple becomes an onion (page 208). These aren't your every-night desserts—though some, like the Fruit Kebabs (page 210), are so easy they could be; in fact, they are exactly what they are meant to be: a special treat before bedtime.

*

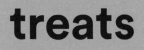

margot and fergus henderson

blood orange upside down cake

Serves 4

For the blood orange caramel:
3 oranges (4 if small)
1 cup (200 g) sugar

For the sponge cake:
4 small or 2 large blood oranges
6 eggs, beaten
3¾ cups (375 g) ground almonds
Generous 3¾ cups (350 g) superfine (caster) sugar
2 teaspoons baking powder
1 teaspoon ground cinnamon
1 teaspoon ground ginger
Pinch of salt

For serving:
4 tablespoons crème fraîche

Blood oranges are one of the most beautiful and vibrant of all the citrus. I [Margot] adore them. I find the flavor more intense than a regular orange and you have all the glamour of the bright carmine color. In this recipe, the blood orange and caramel combine to add a lovely bittersweet tang to your sponge cake. I have to say I'm not the biggest pudding (dessert) maker at home, but my kids love this bright, delicious, and pretty cake. Especially since Hector's winter birthday always falls right in the middle of blood orange season.

•

Make the blood orange caramel
Juice 1 blood orange. Slice the remaining blood oranges into rounds and arrange them, slightly overlapping, on the bottom of a greased cake pan or tarte tatin dish.

In a heavy-bottomed frying pan, gently heat the sugar. Once it starts to melt, slowly swirl the pan around. Once a dark caramel forms, then add the blood orange juice, allowing the mixture to boil and come back together, and pour over the blood orange rounds. Leave to cool.

Make the sponge cake:
Preheat the oven to 325°F (160°C/Gas Mark 3).

Put the blood oranges in a pot and cover with water. Bring to a boil and simmer for 2 hours. (This can be done the day before.) Drain and allow to cool slightly.

⌂ ST. JOHN, ROCHELLE
CANTEEN (LONDON, UK)
•
☺ HECTOR, 26; OWEN,
21; FRANCES, 21

treats
blood orange
upside down cake
↓

dinner
chicken, leek,
and tarragon pie
↳ p. 166

Cut the boiled oranges into chunks and discard the seeds. In a food processor, roughly chop up the oranges, including the peel, and blend until you have a smooth paste. Beat in the eggs, then add the ground almonds, sugar, baking powder, cinnamon, ginger, and salt and blend until well mixed. Pour this mixture over the caramel and oranges (which should have cooled) and bake for 1 hour. Leave to cool for about 30 minutes.

Invert the cake out of the pan, orange-side up, onto a serving plate. Serve with the crème fraîche.

margot and fergus henderson

alex atala

dona palmyra cake

Makes one 9-inch (22 cm) cake

2¼ cups (450 g) granulated sugar
6 eggs, separated
9 oz (250 g) Brazil nuts, grated
3 tablespoons breadcrumbs
1½ teaspoons (10 g) curry powder
2½ teaspoons (10 g) demerara sugar

When I met my wife, Marcia, Joana and Tomás's mom, I also met her family. They used to live in Brasília, the capital of Brazil. Back then, I was introduced to her grandma, Dona Palmyra, who loved to cook and was widely considered the greatest cook of the family. She had this cake recipe and told me I needed to try it. She had won a baking contest using this recipe. She brought me the cake decorated with whipped cream and some questionable cherries. I loved her confidence about her recipe, though I was unsure of the presentation. But when I tried it, I found it was an amazing cake, with extraordinary texture and flavor. That's why I love this recipe and still make it for my children.

•

Preheat the oven to 325°F (160°C/Gas Mark 3).

In a bowl, cream together the granulated sugar and egg yolks until they are pale colored.

In a separate bowl, with an electric mixer, beat the egg whites until stiff peaks form.

Stir the grated nuts into the egg yolk mixture. Fold in the beaten egg whites and the breadcrumbs until incorporated.

<u>treats</u>
dona palmyra cake
↓

<u>dinner</u>
pasta with tomato
and anchovy sauce
↳ p. 144

Scrape the batter into a greased 9-inch (22 cm) cake pan. Transfer to the oven and bake for about 13 minutes.

Let the cake cool in the pan, then invert onto a plate. Combine the curry powder and demerara sugar. With a fine-mesh sieve, sift the mixture over the cake.

pía león and
virgilio martínez

arroz con leche

Serves 4

1 cup (185 g) long-grain rice
Grated zest of 1 orange
Pinch of salt
1 cinnamon stick
8 whole cloves
1½ cups (12 fl oz/355 ml)
evaporated milk
1½ cups (12 fl oz/355 ml)
condensed milk
2 egg yolks
¼ cup (2 fl oz/60 ml) pisco (optional)
Ground cinnamon, for sprinkling

Both of us grew up enjoying this recipe when we were kids. It's common in South America, but we've seen it in Germany where it's called *Milchreis*, and in France, where it's called *riz au lait*. It's a simple, easy-to-make, and quick dessert that relies on the quality of the ingredients. Also, we (including Cristobal) are friends with the dairy farmer, Manuel Choqque of La Vaca Felize. It's always a pleasure to cook with the milk that he delivers.

•

In a medium pot, combine the rice and 4 cups (32 fl oz/945 ml) water and bring to a boil over high heat. Add half of the orange zest, the salt, cinnamon stick, and cloves. Reduce the heat and cook until the rice is tender, about 20 minutes.

Add the evaporated milk and simmer for 10 more minutes. Add the condensed milk and egg yolks and cook for 2 minutes. Remove from the heat. Add the remaining orange zest and the pisco (if using).

Pour it into a square dish and refrigerate to chill.

Serve sprinkled with cinnamon.

MILK

CONDENSED
MILK

EVAPORATED
MILK

treats
arroz con leche
↓

lunch
pumpkin stew with
potatoes and peppers
↳ p. 54

sandra and filip claeys

daddy's crêpes normandy

Serves 4

3 eggs
2 cups (16 fl oz/475 ml) milk
¼ cup (50 g) sugar, plus 8 teaspoons
1⅓ cups (180 g) all-purpose (plain) flour
4 teaspoons unsalted butter, melted
4 teaspoons corn oil
2 apples, peeled, cored, and sliced
Vanilla ice cream, for serving

Every September there is a big gastronomic festival in the city center of Bruges called Kookeet. Lots of chefs in Bruges participate in the event and each year they prepare different things. Five years ago, I [Filip] was crazy enough to make these sweet pancakes for thousands of people over the course of three days. This was also the first year Fleur and Jules were old enough to help out at our booth. They loved it! They helped put the ice cream on top, added the Calvados (which we omit at home), and explained the dish to the guests. Even today, if you ask them what their favorite dessert is, they'll say, "Daddy's Crêpe Normandy . . . without Calvados!"

In a large bowl, mix the together the eggs, milk, ¼ cup (50 g) sugar, and flour.

CREPE

CREEP

Heat a nonstick frying pan over medium heat. Add 1 teaspoon of the melted butter and 1 teaspoon of the corn oil. Place one-quarter of the apples in the pan, heating until each side is golden brown, about 5 minutes per side. Pour one-quarter of the batter over the apples, letting it bake until it becomes golden brown on each side, about 1½ minutes. Add 2 teaspoons of sugar to the pan and flip again, allowing the crêpe to caramelize.

Repeat, adding more butter and oil each time to make 3 more pancakes.

Serve with vanilla ice cream.

CRETE

CRATE

treats

treats
daddy's crêpes normandy
↓

dinner
roast chicken
with artichoke salad
↳ p. 168

floating islands with rose praline

anne-sophie pic

anne-sophie pic

Serves 6

For the custard:
1 cup plus 7 tablespoons (11½ fl oz/
350 ml) whole milk
7 tablespoons (3½ fl oz/100 ml) heavy
(whipping) cream
1 vanilla bean, halved lengthwise
3 oz (80 g) egg yolks (about 4)
½ cup plus 1 tablespoon (70 g)
powdered (icing) sugar

For the islands:
5 oz (150 g) egg whites (about 5)
¾ cup (90 g) powdered sugar
1¼ oz (35 g) pink praline (candied
almonds), crushed
1 teaspoon (2 g) grated lemon zest

Floating islands, or *les îles flottantes*, is a classic French dessert that appears much fancier than it actually is. These little islands of meringue, afloat in a crème anglaise, take only 10 minutes to whip up and bake. (Total time, including allowing the custard to cool, is around 40 minutes.) Here I've included crushed *praline rose* (pink candied almonds), a confection of candied almonds with roots in Lyon. They add a lovely pop of color and crunch to the family favorite dessert.

•

Make the custard:
In a saucepan, combine the milk and cream. Scrape in the vanilla seeds and add the vanilla pod. Heat the milk over medium heat until simmering.

Set up a bowl of ice and water. In a small bowl, mix the egg yolks and the sugar. Pour in a little hot milk, then return everything to the saucepan. Cook slowly over low heat, stirring constantly with a silicone spatula, until the custard thickens and reaches 180°F (83°C). Quickly cool the custard by placing the pan in the ice bath. Remove the vanilla pod when the cream is cold.

Make the islands:
Preheat the oven to 300°F (150°C/Gas Mark 2). Line a baking sheet with parchment paper and set aside.

In a bowl, whisk together the egg whites with the sugar to form soft peaks. Gently mix in half the crushed candied almonds and half the lemon zest.

Spoon the meringue onto the baking sheet into tablespoon-sized mounds. Transfer to the oven and bake for about 5 minutes. Let cool.

treats

🏠 **MAISON PIC
(VALENCE, FRANCE)**

•

☺ **NATHAN, 13**

<u>treats</u>
floating islands
with rose praline

↓

<u>dinner</u>
potato dauphinois
↳ p. 156

<u>To serve:</u>
Pour the custard into small bowls, then place the islands
on top. Sprinkle with the rest of the candied almonds
and lemon zest.

**nick roberts
and
brooke williamson**

fresh plum, black sesame, and vanilla sour belts

Makes 12 ounces (340 g)

5 lb (2.25 kg) plums
¾ cup (150 g) granulated sugar
1 teaspoon salt
2 tablespoons roughly blended (in a spice grinder) black sesame seeds
¼ cup (50 g) superfine (caster) vanilla sugar (you can make your own by stashing your leftover vanilla pods in an airtight container with the sugar for a few days)
2 tablespoons citric acid

Equipment
Dehydrator

A couple of years ago, I [Brooke] got a dehydrator. At the time, my son was in his store-bought fruit leather phase and, as it happens, it was fig season and our garden was full of quickly ripening figs. So I began to experiment with fruit leathers. This version, made from our Santa Rosa plum tree, is our take on sour gummy candy. It's a perfect way to utilize a glut of fruit without any going to waste. And though I use a dehydrator, an oven will do the trick just as well.

•

Preheat the oven to 400°F (200°C/Gas Mark 6).

Wash the plums, cut them in half, and remove the pits (stones).

Lay the halved plums on baking sheets, cut-side up. Place them in the oven for about 15 minutes. Remove from the oven and let cool.

In a blender, blend the plums until smooth (in batches if needed) and pour the finished mixture into a bowl.

Add the granulated sugar and salt to the blended plums and stir well. Add the ground sesame seeds and stir to combine. Pour the purée onto a dehydrator sheet. Use a spoon or spatula to spread the mixture in a completely even layer. You don't want the mixture to be too thin or too thick. It should be anywhere between ⅛–¼ inch (3–6 mm) thick. Place the sheets in the dehydrator set to 135°F (57°C) for 3–4 hours, until the fruit leather is dry to the touch, and no longer super sticky.

treats

⌂ **HUDSON HOUSE,**
THE TRIPEL, PLAYA
PROVISIONS
(LOS ANGELES,
CALIFORNIA, US)
•
☺ **HUDSON, 12**

<u>treats</u>
fresh plum,
black sesame, and
vanilla sour belts

↓

<u>breakfast</u>
egg in a hole
with crispy prosciutto
and broccoli pesto
↳ p. 20

In a large bowl, combine the vanilla sugar and citric acid. Cut the fruit leather into strips and toss in the sour sugar mixture until coated.

Sour belts can be stored at room temperature with a bit of excess sour vanilla sugar mixture for a few months.

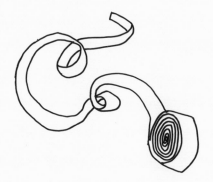

nick roberts and brooke williamson

chocolate-and-apple onion

Serves 4

For the cocoa onion:
6 tablespoons (30 g) unsweetened cocoa powder
½ cup (100 g) sugar
6½ tablespoons (100 ml) orange liqueur
2 crisp apples

For the sauce:
¼ cup (20 g) unsweetened cocoa powder
Generous ¼ cup (60 g) sugar
3 tablespoons (50 ml) orange liqueur

For the banana cake:
Butter, for the baking dish
3 very ripe bananas
1 vanilla bean, split lengthwise
2 eggs
5 tablespoons plus 1 teaspoon (65 g) sugar
3 tablespoons (40 ml) grapeseed oil
¾ cup minus 1 tablespoon (90 g) all-purpose (plain) flour
½ envelope (8 g) baking powder

For serving:
1½ tablespoons (20 g) sugar

Both onions and apples are very Basque ingredients, immediately recognizable to anyone who lives here. Just as I do in Spider Crabs with Sweet Crackers (page 128), in this dessert, I play with that sense of recognition. This chocolate and apple onion looks like half an onion charred a *plancha* but, in fact, it's very long slice of apple coiled together and dusted with cocoa. Both my kids and the clients at Arzak love this sense of whimsy and discovery. It looks like one thing but is another.

●

Make the cocoa onion:
In a saucepan, bring ⅓ cup plus 1 tablespoon (3½ fl oz/ 100 ml) water to a boil. Add ¼ cup (20 g) of the cocoa, a generous ¼ cup (60 g) of the sugar, and the liqueur. Boil together for 1 minute. Then let the liqueur mixture cool.

Carefully peel 1 apple in a single strip. (This takes practice.) Spread out the apple peel—it should be about 6½ feet (2 m) long. Repeat with the second apple.

In a small bowl, combine the remaining 2 tablespoons cocoa and 3 tablespoons sugar and mix well. Then spread and sprinkle the strip of apple peel on both sides with the sugar-cocoa mixture. Coil up the apple peel to achieve the appearance of an onion. Carefully cut in half, as you would an onion, and reserve.

Make the sauce:
In a saucepan, combine ⅓ cup plus 1 tablespoon (3½ fl oz/ 100 ml) water, cocoa, sugar, and orange liqueur and boil for 5 minutes. Cool and reserve.

⌂ **ARZAK**
(SAN SEBASTIÁN, SPAIN)
•
☺ **NORA, 15; MATTEO, 14**

treats
chocolate-and-
apple onion

↓

snacks
spider crabs
with sweet crackers

↳ p. 128

"

When I was growing up, my older sister Maria and I were in a very special situation as the children of chefs. Our father, Juan Mari, was part of the revolution of new Basque cuisine. So when we were six or seven years old, we used to eat all the products and experiments he brought home from the restaurant. We were, I think, the only kids in San Sebastián to be eating Chinese orange, turmeric, curry, ginger, and cacao powder. On the other hand, my father's mother, my grandmother, was a super chef, skilled in traditional Basque recipes. So I grew up on one hand with the avant-garde experimentations of my father and the traditional recipes of his mother. When I was ten or eleven years old, I used to go into my father's kitchen. Then the team was small. Now there are thirty people in the kitchen and it is no place for children. But I do want my own children to know how to cook —even if they never join me in the restaurant—not only for their own health, but so they can improvise dinner and entertain friends.

"

Make the banana cake:
Preheat the oven to 350°F (180°C/Gas Mark 4). Butter an 8 × 8-inch (20 × 20 cm) baking dish.

Place the bananas in a large bowl and scrape in the vanilla seeds. Mash together. In a separate bowl, whisk together the eggs and sugar, then add to the banana mash. Add the grapeseed oil, stirring until incorporated.

In another small bowl, mix the flour and baking powder, then add to the other ingredients, stirring until a batter forms.

Pour into the baking dish. Transfer to the oven and bake until golden brown, about 18 minutes.

Let cool in the baking dish, then cut into ¾ × ¾-inch (2 × 2 cm) squares.

To serve:
Heat a frying pan over medium heat. Dust one side of the cocoa onion in sugar, then place in the frying pan, until caramelized.

Serve with banana biscuits next to the onion, drizzled with sauce around it.

elena arzak

lee anne wong

fruit kebabs

Serves 4

For the kebabs:
1 pineapple, peeled, cored, cut into 1-inch (2.5 cm) chunks
2 quarts (1.4 kg) strawberries, washed and hulled
4–5 bananas, cut into 1-inch (2.5 cm) chunks
1 (16 oz/450 g) bag jumbo marshmallows

For the chocolate sauce:
1 cup (8 fl oz/250 ml) heavy (whipping) cream
¾ cup (170 g) semisweet chocolate chips
⅛ teaspoon salt

Equipment
Eight 8-inch wooden skewers

Rye loves fresh fruit and even more than fruit, he loves putting things on sticks. So this dessert is a no-brainer. We're lucky here in Hawaii to have amazingly fresh fruit, but wherever you are, the genius of the kebab is how variable they can be. You can vary the type of fruit, the frequency of marshmallows, the accoutrements. Rye is crazy for honey so we often finish these with a drizzle, but it could be chocolate sauce or even crushed-up cereal.

•

Make the kebabs:
Alternate fruit chunks and marshmallows on wooden skewers in any desired order. Arrange on a platter.

Make the chocolate sauce:
Heat the heavy cream either in the microwave on medium power for 3 minutes or on the stovetop. Once the cream is hot (just before it boils), remove the cream from the heat and stir in the chocolate chips and salt until they melt and the mixture is smooth.

To serve, drizzle chocolate sauce on the kebabs or serve on the side for dipping.

<u>treats</u>
fruit kebabs
↓

<u>snacks</u>
pork and chive dumplings
↳ p. 116

manoella buffara

cocoa cookies

Makes 24 cookies

1¼ cups (235 g) packed light brown sugar
1½ cups (120 g) finely chopped rolled oats or quick-cooking oats
½ cup (40 g) unsweetened cocoa powder
½ teaspoon baking soda (bicarbonate of soda)
Pinch of salt
Pinch of ground cinnamon
2 tablespoons chia seeds
¼ cup (2 fl oz/60 ml) nondairy milk
⅓ cup (2½ fl oz/75 ml) olive oil or coconut oil
½ cup chopped Brazil nuts, for decoration

All kids love cookies. My kids and these cookies are no exception. In our house, baking these cocoa cookies has already become a tradition, and I allow Helena and Maria to experiment with the recipe and the toppings. Though they're sweet, these cookies are also chock-full of nutritious elements like chia seeds and oats.

•

Preheat the oven to 350°F (180°C/Gas Mark 4).

In a large bowl, stir together the brown sugar, oats, cocoa, baking soda (bicarb), salt, cinnamon, and chia seeds.

In a blender, combine the milk and olive oil until well mixed, about 2 minutes. Pour the liquid into the dry ingredients and mix using a spoon, until a dough is formed. If the dough is dry, adjust with more milk as necessary.

With a greased hand, roll the cookies into 24 small balls. Place on a baking sheet, pressing down gently. Add the nuts and bake until golden brown, about 12 minutes. Remove from the oven and let cool for 5 minutes. Serve.

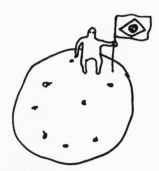

⌂ MANU
(CURITIBA, BRAZIL)
•
☺ HELENA, 5; MARIA, 3

treats
cocoa cookies
↓

snacks
zucchini bread
↳ p. 122

banana balls

palisa anderson

Serves 2

1 lb 5 oz (600 g) very ripe peeled Ducasse bananas
Generous ½ cup (4½ fl oz/130 ml) coconut cream (preferably Kara brand)
½ cup (60 g) tapioca flour
Scant ½ cup (60 g) arrowroot flour
1 tablespoon plus 1 teaspoon salt
2 tablespoons plus 2 teaspoons superfine (caster) raw sugar
2 tablespoons plus 2 teaspoons coconut nectar
6 pandan leaves, washed and cut into 8-inch (20 cm) lengths
9 oz (250 g) shredded fresh coconut*, for serving

Equipment
Double-deck steamer

✾ ◊ 𝄐 ⚘

This dessert, called *khanom gluay*, is made with super-ripe Ducasse bananas—also known as sugar bananas. With their dark, almost black skin, Ducasse bananas are commonly steamed, then scooped out and rolled in coconut. The results are a subtly sweet dessert that isn't too unhealthy. At our restaurant we serve them cut into squares and sprinkled with coconut. But for my kids, I serve them more traditionally, little balls with a coating of coconut flakes. If you can't find Ducasse bananas (but it's worth seeking them out), substitute Finger Lady bananas or even ripe sweet plantains.

•

Bring water to a boil in the bottom of a large double-deck steamer with the steamer insert in place. (If you don't have such a steamer, you could use a large pot with a round cake rack fitted inside. Fill the water up to just the top of the cake rack and not higher.) Place a nonstick cake pan into the steamer insert (or onto the cake rack) and leave it in there until ready to pour the mixture.

In a large bowl, mash the bananas, but not into a smooth purée—leave some varying texture to it—chunky but macerated. Add the coconut cream, tapioca and arrowroot flours, salt, sugar and coconut nectar. Fold gently until it's well incorporated and the sugar has completely dissolved into the mixture. Add the pandan leaves and fold in until evenly distributed through the mixture.

Pour into the cake pan. Don't worry if this seems very runny, it's supposed to be! Cover with a lid and steam for 45 minutes over high heat. Keep adding water to your steamer if it dries out, and if you need to do this, tack on roughly 7 more minutes of cooking time.

⌂ CHAT THAI (SYDNEY, AUSTRALIA)

•

☺ SORAYA, 11; ARTHUR, 10

<u>treats</u>
banana balls

↓

<u>lunch</u>
green papaya salad
↳ p. 68

Uncover and let it sit and cool until you can handle the cake pan. Remove from the steamer and let sit for 30 minutes, for the pan to cool almost entirely or until you feel you can handle the mixture with your clean washed hands.

Get a plate or bowl of the shredded coconut ready.

Pull out and discard all the strips of pandan. Using a tablespoon, scoop out the banana mixture and form into balls, then gently roll through the coconut until generously covered.

Serve immediately, otherwise store in an airtight container somewhere cool (but not the refrigerator, as that will make the balls too firm).

* Best is freshly shredded from a mature coconut. Failing that, look for frozen, but don't used desiccated or dried coconut.

danny bowien

sweet potatoes with milk, peanuts, and maraschino cherries

Serves 2

For the potatoes:
4 small purple sweet potatoes,
well scrubbed

For the garnish:
4 tablespoons condensed milk
4 tablespoons salted roasted peanuts
½ teaspoon salt
8 maraschino cherries, with their
syrup

Mino loves "sweet treats," but I try to limit the amount of sugar he eats. This purple sweet potato "sundae" satisfies his craving for something sweet but doesn't leave me feeling guilty as a parent. Ube, as the purple yam is known, is a relative of taro and is a staple in Asian desserts from the Filipino *ube halaya* and halo-halo to Japanese sweet potato pies.

•

Preheat the oven to 375°F (190°C/Gas Mark 5).

Roast the potatoes whole directly on the oven rack until they're soft to the touch, the skin begins to crack, and their purple juices begin to seep out, about 35 minutes. Carefully remove them from the oven and allow to cool until they're easily handled, about 5 minutes.

Split the potatoes open lengthwise and flatten them. Gently smash their insides with a fork. Garnish each potato half with condensed milk, peanuts, and salt, then top with cherries.

<u>treats</u>
sweet potatoes with milk,
peanuts, and maraschino
cherries
↓

<u>dinner</u>
rice cake soup with
brisket jus and seaweed
\hookrightarrow p. 158

jock zonfrillo

paperbark ice cream and macadamia wafers

Serves 4

For the ice cream:
2 sheets paperbark (about
8 × 11 inches/20 × 28 cm)
Scant ⅔ cup (200 g) honey
2 cups (16 fl oz/475 ml) whole milk
2 cups (16 fl oz/475 ml) heavy
(whipping) cream
⅔ cup (135 g) sugar
8 egg yolks

For the macadamia praline:
10 oz (300 g) macadamia nuts,
toasted and lightly crushed
¾ cup plus 2 tablespoons (300 g)
glucose syrup
1¼ teaspoons salt
1½ cups (300 g) raw sugar

For the wafers:
2 cups (250 g) tipo "00" flour
2 tablespoons (30 ml) grapeseed oil
¾ teaspoon salt

For serving:
Honey, for drizzling

Ⓥ

"

My time spent at home has certainly
changed over the years as I've
grown older. While my career was
undoubtedly the most important
thing when I was younger, I've
happily pushed it to the back seat to
make room and priority for my wife
and children. Family is everything,
and so the first entries in my diary
for the week are for them. Sharing
a meal together every night at the
dinner table is important for us, and
whenever we can, a Sunday lunch is
the best way for us catch up and
round a week off together.

"

Paperbark has a very particular flavor that children seem
to love. Sure, maybe the honey might have something to do
with it, but hey . . . Making ice cream is always a winner
with children and this basic recipe acts a template. It shows
them the method of infusion that lets them begin to create
their own recipes using the same principle.

●

Make the ice cream:
Set up a grill (barbecue) with a charcoal or wood fire.

Brush the paperbark on both sides liberally with honey and
char the paperbark over the fire. Leave to cool, then cut into
small pieces. In a bowl, combine the paperbark and milk*
and let infuse overnight.

Once infused, blitz the bark and milk mixture—do in small
batches as bark clogs the blender. Strain the mixture through
a cheesecloth to ensure all solids have been removed.

In a saucepan, combine the infused milk and cream and heat
to 104°F (40°C).

Meanwhile, set up a large bowl of ice and water. Bring a pan
of water to a simmer (for a double boiler).

In a large heatproof bowl, whisk the sugar and egg yolks
together. Add a small amount of the hot milk/cream mixture
to the egg yolks and sugar, stirring until the mixture is
quite loose. Then add the remaining milk/cream mixture,
set the bowl over the pan of simmering water, and bring
the mixture to 175°F (80°C), constantly stirring to prevent
the eggs from scrambling.

Cool the custard over the ice bath until the mixture reaches room temperature. Taste and season with salt if required. Churn in an ice cream maker until smooth.

Make the macadamia praline:
Line a sheet pan with parchment paper.

In a saucepan, combine the nuts, glucose, 3 tablespoons plus 1 teaspoon (1 ¾ fl oz/50 ml) water, the salt, and the sugar. Bring to a boil and heat to 365°–374°F (185°–190°C). Keep stirring and cooking for 3 minutes. Tip out onto the parchment paper and let cool. Smash to crumbs.

Make the wafers:
In a bowl, stir together the flour, oil, 1⅔ cups (13½ fl oz/ 400 ml) water, and salt.

Set a large nonstick pan over medium-high heat. Brush large strokes of the batter onto the pan. Be artistic while brushing onto the pan; the wafers should peel and curl themselves off the pan. Continue until the batter is all used up.

To serve:
Scoop the ice cream into bowls and add excessive amounts of wafers onto the ice cream, so it looks like a crazy spiky thing of wonderment! Drizzle the wafers lightly with honey and sprinkle liberally with the macadamia praline.

* In the process of straining the infused milk, you will lose several tablespoons, so either top up with fresh milk afterward to come to 2 cups (16 fl oz/475 g), or start out with 2¼ cups (20 fl oz/515 g) milk to account for wastage.

heinz reitbauer

hazelnut puddings with raspberry sauce

Makes 4 puddings

For the hazelnut puddings:
7 tablespoons (100 g) butter, cubed, at room temperature, plus more, melted, for the pudding molds
¾ cup (100 g) all-purpose (plain) flour
1 cup (8 fl oz/250 ml) hay milk or high-quality whole milk
½ teaspoon salt
5 eggs, separated
1 egg yolk
1 tablespoon hazelnut-chocolate spread
2 teaspoons sugar, plus more for dusting the pudding mold
2 teaspoons cornstarch (cornflour)

For the raspberry sauce:
17 oz (500 g) raspberries, crushed
2–3 tablespoons sugar, to taste

For serving:
Vanilla ice cream

Equipment
4 individual steamed pudding molds with lids
Steamer

This dessert—a classic Austrian one that we call *Tag und Nacht*, or Day and Night Pudding—comes from my grandmother Justine, who died recently at the age of 102. Every time I make it I think of her and I make it just the way she did. We use hay milk, or *Heumilch*, which comes from cows fed only hay (and not other substances like corn silage or pellets). But any high-quality organic and farm-fresh milk will do the trick. And if you can't find that, the pudding is still pretty delicious.

•

Make the hazelnut puddings:
In a saucepan, stir together the butter and flour until fully incorporated. Set over medium heat, stir in the milk and salt, and bring to a simmer. Let cool down, then carefully stir in the 6 egg yolks. Separate the batter into two bowls. Add the hazelnut-chocolate spread to one and stir until completely mixed.

Grease 4 individual steamed pudding molds (with lids) with melted butter, dust with a little sugar (the least amount possible), and pour in the hazelnut batter. Set aside in a cool place.

In a bowl, with an electric mixer, beat the 5 egg whites, sugar, and cornstarch (cornflour) until stiff peaks form.

Set up a steamer that will hold the pudding molds.

Fill the pudding molds with alternating layers of meringue and batter. Cover with the lids, transfer to the steamer, and steam until set, 20–25 minutes.

Remove from the steamer, uncover, let cool slightly, and turn out of the molds.

treats
hazelnut puddings
with raspberry sauce
↓

dinner
stuffed cabbage with
potatoes, shallots, and
mustard sauce
↳ p. 172

Make the raspberry sauce:
In a saucepan, combine the raspberries with 2 tablespoons
of the sugar until the raspberries break down into a sauce,
10–12 minutes. Taste and add more sugar if the sauce isn't
sweet enough. As with jam, the texture will be uneven,
with both smaller and bigger pieces. If you prefer a smooth
sauce, strain the raspberries through a sieve and cool down.

To serve:
Serve the puddings with the raspberry sauce and vanilla
ice cream.

andreas caminada

bizochels

Serves 4

3 tablespoons unsalted butter
2⅓ cups (300 g) all-purpose (plain) flour
10 oz (300 g) quark
4 eggs
⅓ cup (50 g) raisins, chopped
Salt and freshly ground black pepper
½ teaspoon ground nutmeg
Fresh mint, chopped
Grated mountain cheese or other hard unpasteurized cow's milk cheese

Equipment
Spaetzle board

"

In the last few years, it's been a big focus of my life to eat more with my family! I work hard and usually have long and busy days. But in 2019, we moved to the very small town of Fürstenau, where our three-star Michelin restaurant and boutique hotel Schloss Schauenstein, as well as our guesthouse Casa Caminada, are located. This means I have my family around almost every day and day-time—from early in the morning, after kindergarten and school, in the after-noon, and at night for a proper family meal before our restaurant service starts. For my wife, Sarah, and me, it is a huge win-win to be able to combine private living with our jobs and have spare time with our sons in between services and daily appointments. We love to garden together with the boys and of course cook. Most days we prefer casual and easy dishes made from seasonal and fresh ingredients. But I also love to cook typical tradi-tional dishes from my home region Graubründen for my family.

"

Bizochels, a sort of spaetzle-like pasta, is a Swiss classic. This is one of my mother's recipes, and I have very fond memories of *Bizochels* growing up. She always added some chopped raisins to her dough, a wonderful variation on the classic. When I make *Bizochels* for my sons, I always prepare a large amount of it, as we all love this simple but tasty dish. Therefore I use a little trick: I fill a syringe with the dough and then pull it over a wire rack that I drape across a pot of boiling water, so that as the strands cross the rack, the thin strands of *Bizochel* tumble into the roiling water below. In Graubünden, the eastern province from which this comes, this dish can skew savory, served with vegetables such as savoy cabbage or Swiss chard, or with bacon and roasted onions. Or they can be sweet, as my mother made them and I do as well, the pasta sweetened by the raisins and balanced by the saltiness of the grated cheese.

•

In a small saucepan, heat the butter over medium-high heat until browned but not burnt. Remove from the heat and set aside.

In a bowl, knead together the flour, quark, and eggs into a light dough. Add the raisins. Season with a pinch each of salt, pepper, and nutmeg.

Bring a large pot of water to a boil.

Place the dough on a spaetzle board and scrape down into long, thin Bizochels. (Or use the syringe trick). Add to the boiling water and cook until the Bizochels float to the surface.

Toss with the brown butter, chopped mint, and grated mountain cheese and serve immediately.

<u>treats</u>
bizochels
↓

<u>lunch</u>
seasonal vegetable salad
↳ p. 72

twisted doughnut, cardamom sugar, and caramel

Serves 4

For the doughnuts:
2 eggs
½ cup (100 g) sugar
7 tablespoons (100 g) unsalted butter
¾ cup plus 2 tablespoons (7 fl oz/
200 ml) whole milk
3¾ cups plus 2 tablespoons (500 g)
all-purpose (plain) flour
2 teaspoons baking powder
½ teaspoon sea salt
Grated zest of 1 lemon

For the cider vinegar caramel:
⅔ cup (120 g) packed dark brown
sugar
⅔ cup (5 fl oz/150 ml) whole milk
⅔ cup (5 fl oz/150 ml) heavy
(whipping) cream
1 tablespoon apple cider vinegar
2 tablespoons (30 ml) fresh lemon
juice
2 tablespoons (15 g) cornstarch
(cornflour)
2 egg yolks
3½ tablespoons (50 g) unsalted
butter, in pieces

For finishing:
Neutral oil, for deep-frying
1 teaspoon (2 g) ground cardamom
¾ cup (150 g) sugar

It's sweet, it's warm, and it has a caramel. There's not much more my kids can ask for! Usually this pastry, called *kleinur*, is made in large batches and kept for a few days, then eaten at room temperature, but they're way better just out of the fryer. They're perfect to get the kids involved in since they're so fun to make. You have to (get to) get your hands dirty. Folding them is fun and, for the older ones, frying them.

•

Make the doughnuts:
In a stand mixer, cream the eggs, sugar, and butter. Add the milk and stir around with clean hands.

In a bowl, whisk together the flour, baking powder, salt, and lemon zest. Mix the dry ingredients into the wet ingredients. Knead the dough until it is smooth and shiny. Cover with plastic wrap (cling film) and refrigerate for 30 minutes.

Make the cider vinegar caramel:
In a large pot, stir together the brown sugar, milk, cream, butter, vinegar, lemon juice, and cornstarch (cornflour). Set over medium heat and stir constantly until the mixture is very thick. Add a bit of the hot mixture to the egg yolks to temper them, then mix everything together. Let cool before serving.

To finish:
Roll the dough out to ¼-inch (6 mm) thickness and cut into 1-inch (2.5 cm) "rhombus" squares (diamonds). Make a slit down the center of the diamond, going the long way, and stopping well short of both ends. Take one of the ends and push it through the slit and pull it back to its original position—sort of like making a knot.

<u>treats</u>
twisted doughnut,
cardamom sugar,
and caramel
↓

<u>dinner</u>
icelandic fish stew
with rye bread
↳ p. 180

Pour 3 inches (7.5 cm) oil into a deep heavy pot or deep fryer. Heat the oil to 300°F (150°C).

Meanwhile, in a spice grinder combine the cardamom and sugar and blitz to a powder. Transfer to a shallow bowl.

Working in batches, drop the doughnuts into the hot oil and fry until golden brown, about 4 minutes. Toss in the cardamom sugar.

Serve the kleinur hot alongside the caramel for dipping.

greek doughnuts with honey and yogurt

<u>Serves 4</u>

<u>For the syrup:</u>
1 cup (200 g) sugar
1 slice lemon
1 tablespoon honey

<u>For the dough:</u>
1 cup plus 3 tablespoons (9½ fl oz/ 280 ml) warm (but not hot) water
Scant 3 teaspoons (9 g) active dry yeast
1 tablespoon honey
Pinch of salt
1½ cups (200 g) all-purpose (plain) flour
7 tablespoons (50 g) corn flour
Sunflower oil, for deep-frying

<u>For serving:</u>
Ground cinnamon
Honey
½ cup (50 g) crushed walnuts

Almost every culture has some sort of fried dough dessert. The Spaniards have *buñuelos*, the French have beignets, the Portuguese have *sonhos*, and we Greeks have *loukoumades*. We may have borrowed the name from the Turkish *lokma*, but the first such sweet was likely from the Romans, making it one of the earliest known desserts in the world. Here in Greece, *loukoumades* were given to winners in the Olympic games. My sons, Matthew and Manos, love eating these treats all year round but especially on New Year's Eve, when we stick a coin in one dough ball and whoever finds it is guaranteed luck for the next year. Don't hesitate to try them with different toppings such as dark chocolate and almonds, white chocolate and strawberries, sugar and lemon, nutmeg, and maple syrup and pistachio.

•

<u>Make the syrup:</u>
In a saucepan, combine the sugar, 1 cup (8 fl oz/250 ml) water, lemon, and honey and bring to a boil. Remove from the heat and transfer to another pan to cool faster. (The syrup needs to be completely cool when you put the doughnuts into it.)

<u>Make the dough:</u>
In a bowl, stir together the water, yeast, honey, salt, all-purpose (plain) flour, and corn flour. Stir with a spoon until it becomes a thick batter. Cover the bowl with plastic wrap (cling film) and let it rise in a warm and dry environment for 30–45 minutes.

Pour 3 inches (7.5 cm) sunflower oil into a deep heavy pan. Heat over medium heat to 320°F (160°C).

Meanwhile, fill a glass high enough with sunflower oil that you can submerge the bowl of a teaspoon in it. This is to coat the spoon so the dough doesn't stick to it as you form the doughnuts. Line a plate with paper towels (this is for the doughnuts to drain).

When ready to fry, put your hand into the bowl of dough and grab some dough with your nondominant hand. Start to close it in your hand so the dough begins to overflow between the index finger and the thumb. Take the oiled teaspoon in the other hand and use it to scoop off spoons of the dough, letting them fall into the hot oil. Continue "cutting" small loukoumades, re-oiling the spoon as you go, taking care not to crowd the pan.

After they have cooked on one side, use a slotted spoon to flip them over and let them cook on the other side. Fry for a few minutes until lightly browned, remove from the pan, and place on the paper towels to drain. Continue with more batches, letting the oil come back to temperature each time.

Leave them on the plate for a few minutes. Then reheat the oil and fry them once more in hot oil until they get a good color and become crispy. Remove from the pan, let drain for a few moments, and toss in the cooled syrup. To finish, sprinkle with cinnamon, honey, and walnuts and serve.

chef biographies

palisa anderson

Chat Thai, the award-winning Sydney restaurant, was founded in 1989 by Palisa Anderson's mother, Amy Chanta. Since then, the business has expanded its operations to nine restaurants, a grocery store, a travel agency, and a farm. Palisa joined the business after spending a decade traveling the world. Today her role ranges from menu creation to selecting the herbs, fruits, and vegetables of her organically certified farm Boon Luck Farm Organics, which supplied the produce for Noma's Sydney pop-up.

karena armstrong

Prior to opening The Salopian Inn in Southern Australia's McLaren Vale, Armstrong worked in some of the country's most prestigious kitchens, including with Karen Martini at the Melbourne Wine Room and with Kylie Kwong at Billy Kwong. At the Salopian Inn, housed in a 150-year-old stone building set amid a vast kitchen garden, Armstrong focuses her tasting menu on championing local ingredients.

elena arzak

Elena Arzak is the fourth-generation chef and owner of the three-Michelin-star Arzak Restaurant in San Sebastián, Spain. After studying at some of the world's best restaurants, Arzak joined her father as the pioneer of New Basque cuisines in 1996, working her way up to co-chef. Arzak is the recipient of many honors including the Chef de l'Avenir Award in 2001 and World's Best Female Chef Award in 2012.

reem assil

Reem Assil is a Palestinian-Syrian chef based in the San Francisco Bay area. After a decade as a labor-and-community organizer, she opened Reem's California, a nationally acclaimed restaurant with locations in San Francisco and Fruitvale (a neighborhood of Oakland), inspired by her passion for Arab street corner bakeries and the vibrant communities that surround them. In 2018, with chef Daniel Patterson, Assil debuted Dyafa, a more upscale restaurant in San Francisco. That year, Reem's was named a Restaurant of the Year by *Food & Wine* magazine.

alex atala

Alex Atala is Brazil's best-known chef and the champion of his nation's cuisine. His São Paulo restaurant, D.O.M., is #10 on the Latin America's 50 Best Restaurants list. In addition to D.O.M., Atala's other ventures include Dalva e Dito, Restaurante Bio, and the nonprofit ATÁ. Atala was featured in the second season of *Chef's Table*. He is the author of *D.O.M.: Rediscovering Brazilian Ingredients*.

danny bowien

In 2010, Danny Bowien, who was born in South Korea and adopted by an American family in Oklahoma City, opened the original Mission Chinese Food in San Francisco. It was named the second Best New Restaurant in America by *Bon Appétit*. In 2013, Bowien was awarded Rising Star Chef by the James Beard Foundation. After leaving San Francisco in 2012, Bowien opened a stand-alone Mission Chinese Food in New York City's Lower East Side. In 2017, Bowien was the subject of the sixth season of the PBS show *The Mind of a Chef*.

sean brock

In 2010, Sean Brock, chef and owner of Husk, in Charleston, South Carolina, won the James Beard Award for Best Chef Southeast. He hosted Season 2 of the television show *The Mind of a Chef*, produced by Anthony Bourdain, and was featured on Season 6 of *Chef's Table*. After leaving Husk in 2019, Brock opened his flagship restaurant Audrey in East Nashville, Tennessee. He is the author of the cookbooks *Heritage* and *South*.

manoella buffara

Manoella Buffara is the Executive Chef and owner of Manu in Curitiba, Brazil, which has received critical acclaim and was recognized on Latin America's 50 Best Restaurants list. Buffara's eleven-course tasting menu celebrates the culture and produce unique to the region of Paraná.

andreas caminada

In 2003, at only twenty-six years old, Andreas Caminada took over as chef at Schloss Schauenstein, a castle restaurant in Fürstenau, a small town in eastern Switzerland. Shortly thereafter, the restaurant earned three Michelin stars and nineteen Gault Millau points and appeared on the World's 50 Best Restaurants list. Caminada has expanded into numerous restaurants as well as establishing the Uccelin Foundation, which promotes and fosters young culinary talent in Switzerland.

jeremy charles

Newfoundland chef Jeremy Charles and his restaurant Raymonds are both frequently ranked as Canada's best chef and restaurant, respectively. The restaurant, located in downtown, relies heavily on the natural bounty of Newfoundland and Labrador, often including moose he has hunted. He is the author of *Wildness: An Ode to Newfoundland and Labrador*.

sandra and filip claeys

In a former hunting lodge nestled into a modern garden just outside of Bruges, Belgium, Filip and Sandra Claeys present modern Flemish fine dining, drawing their ingredients from Belgian fisheries and local farmers. Opened in 2006, the restaurant was awarded two Michelin stars and four toques from Gault Millau.

margarita forés

Named Asia's Best Female Chef by Asia's 50 Best Restaurants in 2016, Margarita Forés runs several of the Philippines' most well-regarded fine-dining restaurants, including Cibo, Lusso, Grace Park, and Las Casas Manila. Having studied and lived in Italy, Forés continues to reimagine Italian classics using local ingredients, was knighted by the Italian government, and, in 2019, named a United Nations Ambassador for Gastronomic Tourism. Her restaurants are among myriad entrepreneurial endeavors, which include a catering company, a floral artistry line, and a tableware collection.

suzanne goin and david lentz

In 1998, Los Angeles–born Suzanne Goin took her hometown restaurant world by storm opening Lucques, a French-inspired restaurant opened with business partner Caroline Styne. Since then, Goin has opened A.O.C., Tavern, and the Larder at Maple Drive among others, has written iconic cookbooks such as *Sunday Suppers at Lucques*, and won many awards, including James Beard Best Chef California in 2016. For over fifteen years, her husband, Baltimore native David Lentz, was the chef and co-owner with Goin of the seafood-centric gastropub The Hungry Cat, which closed in 2019.

will goldfarb

In 2008, after years atop New York City's restaurant scene, pastry chef Will Goldfarb relocated his avant-garde dessert restaurant Room 4 Dessert to Ubud, Bali. Goldfarb, who trained under chefs including Ferran Adrià, Tetsuya Wakuda, and Masaharu Morimoto, as well as winning the James Beard Award for Best Pastry Chef, reinvented the restaurant in its jungle setting while pushing the envelope for what constitutes dessert. In 2019, he was featured on *Chef's Table: Pastry*. He is the author of *Room for Dessert*.

adeline grattard

Adeline Grattard is the chef and owner of yam'Tcha in Paris. After working in the kitchen at the iconic restaurant l'Astrance, Grattard moved to Hong Kong to work at Bo Innovation restaurant. She returned to Paris with her husband, Chi Wah Chan, to open yam'Tcha, a fine-dining restaurant, which combines French and Chinese culinary culture. Yam'Tcha received its first Michelin star in 2009, while Grattard, profiled on *Chef's Table*, won Omnivore Innovation Chef in 2019.

jocelyn guest and erika nakamura

Tokyo-born Erika Nakamura and Jocelyn Guest of Virginia co-founded the New York City whole-animal butcher shop White Gold in 2016, earning two stars from the *New York Times*. In 2018, the couple left the restaurant and the city to establish J&E Small Goods, an artisanal retail butchery in upstate New York.

rodolfo guzmán

After working with Andoni Luis Aduriz at Mugaritz in Spain, Chilean chef Rodolfo Guzmán opened Boragó in 2009 in Santiago, Chile. An early and ardent proponent of Chilean cuisine, Boragó worked with the Mapuche (the Indigenous inhabitants of Chile and Argentina) as well as chemistry and biology professors at the local university to rediscover the national larder. Today, Guzmán works with over two hundred local purveyors to source his ingredients, as well as from his own orchard. The restaurant is #26 on the World's 50 Best Restaurants list. He is the author of *Boragó: Coming from the South*.

margot and fergus henderson

British-born Fergus Henderson is among the most lauded British chefs of his generation and a pioneer of head-to-tail dining, a philosophy promulgated through his restaurant St. John in London. New Zealand–born Margot Henderson is a founder of the caterer Arnold & Henderson and chef of Rochelle Canteen, a revered restaurant in London. Among Fergus's books are *Beyond Nose to Tail* and *The Book of St. John*; among Margot's is *You're All Invited: Margot's Recipes for Entertaining*.

edouardo jordan

Originally from Florida, Jordan worked at The French Laundry in Healdsburg, California, Per Se and Lincoln Ristorante in New York, as well as Matt Dillon's Sitka & Spruce. He then opened the Italian-inflected Salare in 2015 and in 2017, JuneBaby, one of the first fine-dining restaurants to celebrate Black diasporic cuisine. In 2018, Jordan won the James Beard Award for Best Chef, the first Black chef to do so, while his first restaurant, Salare, won Best New Restaurant.

najat kaanache

Born in San Sebastián, Spain, Najat Kaanache worked in the kitchens of Noma, The French Laundry, and el Bulli before opening Nur, a fine-dining restaurant in the medina of Fez, Morocco, in 2016. Since then the restaurant, which means "light" in Arabic, has been named the best restaurant in Morocco. Kaanache is the author of the cookbook *Najat* and host of Canal Cocina's *Cocina Marroquí*.

asma khan

Asma Khan is the chef and owner of Darjeeling Express in London. She moved to Cambridge from her native Calcutta in 1991. After earning her PhD in Law at King's College London, she began her culinary career with a supper club in her home in 2012. Darjeeling Express opened its doors in 2017 to widespread acclaim. In 2019, Khan became the first British chef featured on *Chef's Table*.

beverly kim and johnny clark

Beverly Kim and Johnny Clark opened Parachute, a Korean American restaurant in Chicago's Avondale neighborhood in 2014. The restaurant earned a Michelin star in 2015. In 2019, they opened a fine dining restaurant called Wherewithall, welcomed their third child, and jointly won the James Beard Awards for Best Great Lakes Chef.

james knappett and sandia chang

Sandia Chang of Los Angeles met British-born chef James Knappett in the kitchen of Thomas Keller's Per Se in New York, where they were both working. The fine-dining chefs returned to the UK in 2012 to open Bubbledogs, a champagne-and-hot dog bar and Kitchen Table, a two-Michelin-star tasting menu restaurant in its back room.

angelos lantos

Hailing from north of the Peloponnese, Angelos Lantos began his work in restaurants as a waiter, before gaining kitchen experience in some of Greece's most renowned restaurants. In 2005 he joined Spondi, an Athenian gastronomic institution, and took over from his mentor, French chef Arnaud Bignon, in 2013. That year Lantos was the first Greek chef to be awarded two Michelin stars.

summer le

A food blogger and tour operator exploring the bounty of Central Vietnamese cuisine, Summer Le opened Nén, a modern Vietnamese restaurant, in her hometown of Da Nang in 2017. Le and her team grow the majority of their produce on the restaurant's rooftop farm and source the seafood from local fisherman along the Han River. A renowned showcase for rare and endangered ingredients, the restaurant has featured on the 50 Best Discovery list and gained an international following.

pía león and virgilio martínez

Peru's Pía León and Virgilio Martínez are the co-owners and chefs at Central, Peru's most esteemed restaurant and ranked #6 on the World's 50 Best Restaurants list. Champions of indigenous ingredients, the couple continue their mission with Kjolle, a Lima restaurant led by León, and Mil, in Cusco. Martínez is the author of *Central*.

walter and margarita manzke

After meeting in the kitchen of legendary chef Joachim Splichal at Los Angeles's Patina, Walter and Margarita Manzke opened their first bakery, Wildflour Bakery and Café in the Philippines, where Margarita was born and raised. In 2014, the Manzkes opened the French restaurant République in Los Angeles. The couple have also opened Sari Sari Store and Petty Cash Taqueria, both in Los Angeles, and fifteen locations of Wildflour in the Philippines.

gísli matt

Gísli Matt was born in Heimaey in Vestmannaeyjar (Westman Islands) of Iceland to a family of fishermen and cooks. He began working in kitchens in 2007 and built his restaurant, Slippurinn, from scratch with the help of his family. The restaurant, which opened in 2012 in a former machinery workshop in Heimaey, is open just four months a year and has come to embody the vanguard of new Icelandic cuisine. In 2017, Matt expanded with SKÁL, a more casual food hall in Reykjavik.

jp mcmahon

JP McMahon, a chef and restaurateur, is the director of Ireland's EatGalway Restaurant Group, which includes the Michelin-starred Aniar, Tartare (a natural wine bar), and the tapas bar Cava Bodega. He is also founder of Food on the Edge, an annual food conference in Galway. He writes a weekly column for the *Irish Times* and is the author of *The Irish Cookbook*.

bonnie morales

The daughter of Soviet immigrants, Morales studied French cuisine and cooked in restaurants including Chicago's Tru. She then returned to her roots in 2014 by opening Kachka in Portland, Oregon—today widely considered the best Russian restaurant in the United States. She is the author of *Kachka: A Return to Russian Cooking*.

nompumelelo mqwebu

Nompumelelo Mqwebu is a South African chef, founder of the Mzansi International Culinary Festival, and owner of Kumyoli Culinary Experiences, a tour company that focuses on authentic African cuisine with indigenous ingredients. She is the author of the cookbook *Through the Eyes of an African Chef*.

vladimir mukhin

Born in a small town in southern Russia, Vladimir Mukhin opened White Rabbit on the sixteenth floor of an office tower in Moscow in 2012. A fifth-generation chef, Mukhin is passionate about presenting the full potential of Russian cuisine, a pursuit captured in Season 3 of Netflix's *Chef's Table*. Ranked #13 on the World's 50 Best Restaurants list, White Rabbit is now joined by a score of other restaurants, also co-owned by Mukhin, including the critically acclaimed Selfie.

yoshihiro narisawa

One of Japan's most renowned chefs, Yoshihiro Narisawa is the chef and owner of Narisawa. Originally called Les Créations de Narisawa—a nod to his time in the kitchens of Paul Bocuse and Joël Robuchon—the restaurant opened in 2003. The menu embodies the chef's vision of "innovative *satoyama* cuisine," a cuisine bred of forests and foothills. The restaurant is #22 on the World's 50 Best Restaurants list.

anne-sophie pic

Anne-Sophie Pic is the third-generation chef of Maison Pic, a three-Michelin-star restaurant in Valence, in the south of France. After living and studying abroad, Pic returned to the restaurant in 1992, shortly before her father died. After the restaurant lost its third Michelin star in 1995, Pic took over in 1997 and spent the next ten years earning it back. Among her other restaurants are La Dame de Pic in London and Restaurant Anne-Sophie Pic in Lausanne, Switzerland. In 2011, she was both awarded World's Best Female Chef and named to France's Legion of Honor.

elisabeth prueitt

In 2002, with her then-husband Chad Robertson, Elisabeth Prueitt founded San Francisco's Tartine Bakery, which has since expanded to include an empire of well-regarded bakeries including Tartine Manufactory and Manufactory Coffee. In 2008, she won the James Beard Award for Best Pastry Chef in America. With Chad Robertson, she is the co-author of *Tartine, Tartine All Day*, and *Tartine: A Classic Revisited*.

heinz reitbauer

Heinz Reitbauer is the second-generation owner and chef of Steirereck, a fine-dining restaurant featuring ingredients from southeastern Austria's Styrian region. Thanks to Reitbauer's passion for imaginative and deeply thoughtful preparations, the restaurant, located in a mirrored glass palace in Vienna's Stadtpark, is #17 on the World's 50 Best Restaurants list.

elena reygadas
Born and raised in Mexico City, Elena Reygadas is the chef and owner of Rosetta, Panadería Rosetta, Lardo, and Café Nin, all in Mexico City. Rosetta, her first restaurant and located in a mansion in the Roma Norte neighborhood, is the cornerstone of her gastronomic empire and widely considered the vanguard of Mexican fine dining. In 2014, Reygadas was named Latin America's Best Female Chef. She is the author of the cookbook *Rosetta*.

jonathan rhodes
A former United States Marine, Jonathan "Jonny" Rhodes is the award-winning chef behind Indigo, a fine-dining restaurant at the forefront of Black diasporic cuisine in Houston, Texas. With just thirteen seats, the restaurant focuses on Indigenous and Black foodways, has a mission grounded in social justice, and was named one of *Time* magazine's 100 World's Greatest Places.

reuben riffel
South African chef Reuben Riffel was born in Franschhoek, South Africa. After opening a brasserie in London, in 2004, he returned to South Africa, to Johannesburg, to open Reuben's, which won the Eat Out Restaurant Award for Restaurant of the Year, with Riffel winning Best Chef of the Year. Riffel has opened four more restaurants, is the author of four cookbooks, served as a judge of *MasterChef South Africa*, and hosted the cooking show *5 Sterre met Reuben*.

nick roberts and brooke williamson
After working at Michael's in Santa Monica, California, and Daniel in New York, Brooke Williamson and her husband, Nick Roberts, an alum of the kitchens of Alain Ducasse and Daniel Boulud, opened Hudson House in Redondo Beach, California. The pair have since expanded to open Playa Provisions and The Tripel. Williamson is the winner of Season 14 of the television show *Top Chef*.

ana roš
In 2002, Ana Roš gave up a career path as a diplomat to take over the restaurant of her husband's family, Hiša Franko. Since then, the self-taught Roš has transformed the restaurant in Slovenia's Soča Valley into a world-renowned dining destination. Through appearances on *Chef's Table* as well as numerous accolades, including being ranked on the World's 50 Best Restaurants list and winning the World's Best Female Chef award, Roš has redefined and elevated Slovenian cuisine. She is the author of *Ana Roš: Sun and Rain*.

daniel rose and marie-aude rose
American-born chef Daniel Rose operates Le Bourse et La Vie and Chez la Vieille in Paris and New York's Le Coucou. French-born Marie-Aude Rose is the chef of New York's lauded Le Mercerie. The family splits their time between New York and Paris.

didem şenol
After graduating in psychology from Koç University, Istanbul, Şenol moved to New York to study at the French Culinary Institute. After working in some of New York's best kitchens—including Eleven Madison Park—she returned to Turkey and in 2005 opened her first restaurant, Lokanta Maya, which earned her Best Chef at the Time Out Istanbul Awards. Her second restaurant, Gram, which focuses on local and seasonal ingredients, opened in 2012 and has since expanded to three locations.

ben shewry

Attica, the Melbourne restaurant that Ben Shewry took over in 2005, is routinely ranked among the world's best. Shewry, the New Zealand–born chef, was among the inaugural crop of chefs profiled in the first season of Netflix's *Chef's Table* and is widely credited for championing indigenous ingredients within a fine-dining context in Australasia. He is the author of *Origin: The Food of Ben Shewry*.

duangporn songvisava and dylan jones

Thai-born Duangporn "Bo" Songvisava and her Australian-born husband, Dylan Jones, opened Bo.lan in a historic Bangkok villa in 2009. In 2013, Songvisava was named Asia's Best Female Chef by Asia's 50 Best Restaurants and was featured on the television program *Chef's Table*. Bo.lan continues to push Thai cuisine forward with a focus on creativity and sustainability.

max strohe and ilona scholl

Max Strohe and Ilona Scholl's restaurant tulus lotrek opened in Berlin-Kreuzberg in 2015, with an emphasis on Strohe's imaginative flavor combinations and Scholl's hospitality. In 2016, Strohe was named Berlin's Rising Star Chef by Berlin Master Chefs and the restaurant earned its first Michelin star in 2017, followed by inclusion in the 50 Best Discovery series in 2019.

pierre thiam

Born and raised in Dakar, Senegal, Pierre Thiam is the executive chef of the award-winning restaurant NOK by Alára in Lagos, Nigeria, and Teranga, a fast-casual food chain in New York City. His company Yolélé Foods advocates for smallholder farmers in the Sahel by opening new markets for crops grown in Africa. He is the author of *The Fonio Cookbook*.

kwang uh and mina park

Kwang Uh and Mina Park met in the temple of renowned South Korean Zen chef Jeong Kwan. In 2015, Kwang Uh opened the modern Korean-American restaurant Baroo, earning numerous accolades and a coveted Jonathan Gold rave review in the *Los Angeles Times*. After numerous iterations, including a hiatus, the couple opened Shiku, located in Los Angeles's Grand Central Market, in 2019, and Baroo 2.0 in 2020.

mickael viljanen

Mickael Viljanen was born in Stockholm, Sweden, and moved to the west coast of Finland, where he started cooking from an early age. He has been working in kitchens since he was fourteen years old. He has traveled for work extensively across Europe and Asia. Viljanen is the executive chef of the two-Michelin-star restaurant The Greenhouse in Dublin, where he has worked since 2012.

lee anne wong

After stints in the New York kitchens of Marcus Samuelsson's Aquavit and Jean-Georges Vongerichten's Restaurant 66, a position as an executive chef at the French Culinary Institute, and a series of appearances on *Top Chef*, New York native Lee Anne Wong relocated to Honolulu, Hawaii, to open Koko Head Cafe. The restaurant opened in 2014 and has become one of Honolulu's top brunch spots. Wong is the author of *Dumplings All Day Wong*.

claudette zepeda-wilkins

Claudette Zepeda-Wilkins is best known as the executive chef behind El Jardín, a Mexican restaurant in San Diego, California. During her tenure, the restaurant was included as an *Esquire* 2018 Best New Restaurant and earned a Michelin Bib Gourmand. In 2018, Zepeda-Wilkins was named Chef of the Year by Eater San Diego

and *San Diego Union-Tribune*. Her most
recent restaurant, VAGA at Alila Marea,
opened in 2020.

jock zonfrillo
Jock Zonfrillo's Adelaide restaurant,
Restaurant Orana, opened in 2007 and
was awarded Australian Restaurant of the
Year in 2018 and 2019. At Orana, Zonfrillo,
who was born in Scotland of Italian ancestry,
conveys Australia's modern gastronomic
identity by using indigenous ingredients over
a sixteen-course menu at only six tables.
In 2020, he was a judge on the television
series *MasterChef Australia*.

index

Recipe Notes:
All butter is salted, unless otherwise specified.

All pepper is freshly ground black pepper, unless otherwise specified.

All eggs are large, unless otherwise specified.

All sugar is superfine (caster) sugar, unless otherwise specified.

Individual vegetables and fruits, such as carrots and apples, are assumed to be medium, unless otherwise specified.

Exercise a high level of caution when following recipes involving any potentially hazardous activity, including the use of high temperatures, open flames and when deep-frying. In particular, when deep-frying, add food carefully to avoid splashing, wear long sleeves and never leave the pan unattended.

Cooking times are for guidance only. If using a fan (convection) oven, follow the manufacturer's instructions concerning the oven temperatures.

Some recipes include lightly cooked eggs, meat and fish, and fermented products. These should be avoided by the elderly, infants, pregnant women, convalescents, and anyone with an impaired immune system.

Exercise caution when making fermented products, ensuring all equipment is spotlessly clean, and seek expert advice if in any doubt.

All herbs, shoots, flowers, berries, seeds and vegetables should be picked fresh from a clean source. Exercise caution when foraging for ingredients. Any foraged ingredients should only be eaten if an expert has deemed them safe to eat.

When no quantity is specified, for example of oils, salts and herbs used for finishing dishes, quantities are discretionary and flexible

All spoon and cup measurements are level, unless otherwise stated. 1 teaspoon = 5 ml; 1 tablespoon = 15 ml. Australian standard tablespoons are 20 ml, so Australian readers are advised to use 3 teaspoons in place of 1 tablespoon when measuring small quantities.

Author Acknowledgments:
First of all, I'd like to thank my mother, Marcia Lieberman. You know, I wasn't (and am not) a fan of her Applesauce Meatloaf or Company Creamed Tuna, but by golly she tried. Now, as a working parent, I know how hard it must have been. So, thanks, Ma, for keeping me fed and, you know, being a wonderful mother. This kind of book can only happen with the unmatched generosity of the contributing chefs who have graciously contributed their recipes, finding the time for this extra project on top of running some of the world's best restaurants and taking care of their own families. So my deepest gratitude goes to the chefs who have participated. Nor would this book have taken form had not Emily Takoudes at Phaidon had the faith, patience, and vision to see it to fruition. Finally, I would be remiss not to thank my own children, Augustus and Achilles Heeren Stein, for whom it has (sometimes) been a pleasure to cook, but for whom it has been the greatest joy in my life to parent.

Author Bio:
Joshua David Stein is the author of many cookbooks and children's books. He is the co-author of *Notes from a Young Black Chef*, with Kwame Onwuachi, *The Nom Wah Cookbook* with Wilson Tang, *Il Buco* with Donna Lennard, and *Food & Beer* with Daniel Burns and Jeppe Jarnit-Bjergsø. Formerly the editor-at-large at the parenting site Fatherly, he is also the author of *To Me, He Was Just Dad*. Among his children's books are *Can I Eat That?*, *What's Cooking?*, *Brick: Who Found Herself in Architecture*, *Can You Eat?*, *The Ball Book*, and *The Invisible Alphabet*. Stein lives in Brooklyn, New York, with his sons, Auggie and Achilles.

Phaidon Press Limited
2 Cooperage Yard
London E15 2QR

Phaidon Press Inc.
65 Bleecker Street
New York, NY 10012

phaidon.com

First published 2021
© 2021 Phaidon Press Limited
Text and illustrations © Joshua David Stein

ISBN 978 1 83866 252 3

A CIP catalogue record for this book is available from the British Library and the Library of Congress.

Editor: Emily Takoudes
Production Controller: Gif Jittiwutikarn

Designed by Julia Hasting
Illustrations by Joshua David Stein

Printed in China

The publisher would like to thank all of the chefs for their participation and use of their photographs; also to Lesley Malkin, João Mota, Elizabeth Parson, Sarah Scott, Albino Tavares, and Kate Slate.